Living
Hinduism

Living Hinduism

Scriptures
Philosophy
Practices

SAMARPAN

NIYOGI
BOOKS

Published by
NIYOGI BOOKS
Block D, Building No. 77,
Okhla Industrial Area, Phase-I,
New Delhi-110 020, INDIA
Tel: 91-11-26816301, 26818960
Email: niyogibooks@gmail.com
Website: www.niyogibooksindia.com

Text © Samarpan

Editor: Jayalakshmi Sengupta
Design: Shraboni Roy

ISBN: 978-93-85285-80-6
Publication: 2017

Printed at: Niyogi Offset Pvt. Ltd., New Delhi, India

Dedicated to

Srimat Swami Atmapriyananda ji

*without whose kind support none of my writings would have
been possible*

Contents

❖

Preface 9

❖

❖

❖

❖

❖

Preface

Perception matters in religion, as in everything else. A religion's essence, as seen by its practitioners and preachers, may lie in peace, forgiveness, unity, etc.; but outsiders often judge it for its apparent practices, say, conversion, dogmatism, vegetarianism, and such.

Hindu dharma, or simply Hinduism, beats every other religion when it comes to misperception. Its core is missed by outsiders and also by its practitioners. Most Hindus associate their religion with gods, goddesses, rituals, temples, and charlatans, while outsiders think of it as a religion of cows, cowardice, and castes. Unlucky foreigners also link it with cheats and *chara*s. And yet, none of these has any importance in Hinduism.

The reason for this wrong perception is that the attackers of Hinduism usually have only a fleeting knowledge of it, acquired mostly through biased writings, and the practising Hindus rarely ever see the source books. It is a sad fact about Hinduism that nearly the entire population of Hindus have only simplistic ideas about this majestic religion whose sweep once reached from the borders of Iran to Indonesia, and from China to Sri Lanka.

Sages and saints have been born in the Hindu tradition at regular intervals throughout its history. Even in the 19th and

20th centuries we had greats like Dayanada Saraswati, Sri Ramakrishna, Swami Vivekananda, and Sri Raman Maharshi, who contributed mightily through their spiritual achievements to show what Hindu dharma is truly about. But the stocky Indian inertia makes people forget the greatness and intensity of their contribution, and they soon retreat to the age old Pin-zones of their vegetative beliefs and rituals.

This work is a modest attempt at presenting Hinduism the way it is, and the way it should be perceived. It discusses the basics of this grand old religion that has played mother to three major religions—Buddhism, Jainism, and Sikhism, and has left deep influences on Zoroastrianism and Christianity.

One problem in discussing Hinduism is that it is both a religion and a society. This complicates matters, since the practices of the Hindu society and Hindu religion get mixed up. For example, caste was a social system to safeguard the interests of particular groups with common ancestry. It had nothing to do with religion, but over the years it has been wrongly identified as an integral part of Hinduism, the religion. Similarly, putting on the sacred thread was a religious practice, but it later got transformed into a social custom for the upper caste Hindus. In modern times, marriages have moved from being the religious act it used to be, to becoming a social institution where one marries for reasons other than spiritual growth.

The aim of this work is to present Hinduism, the religion, and so, it does not discuss the social aspects and issues. The book is divided into four parts: the first one gives a brief outline of Hinduism, the second part gives an overview of its scriptures, the third one discusses the philosophies, and the last section looks at the future Hinduism.

Efforts have been made to keep things simple and easy. Even then, readers may find some of the ideas a bit difficult in the first reading. Sorry about that.

This work is a product of long years of studying, learning, and practising. Care has been taken to present the facts as they are, but even then, chances of mistakes are always there. Sincere apologies for that.

'Eternal amidst non-eternal, consciousness amidst intelligence, substratum of everything, He fulfils the desires of all—know him within your heart to attain everlasting peace.'

— *Kathopanishad*

HINDUISM

Religion and Spirituality

The most common, and hence crude, understanding about religion is that there is some God, sitting high up in the clouds, who controls things from there for us. When we pray to him, he, like an obedient robot or a loving grandpa, sets wheels moving in our favour, which we call a miracle, and if we do not get a favourable response, we are free to curse him and his insensibility. He favours the devoted, and hurts the bad. So if one offers something to him, the gears of his favour get greased.

There can never be a more elementary understanding of religion than this. Religion runs at much deeper levels.

Religion is characterised by the struggle to attain universal existence. It is a journey from a personalised existence, limited by time and space, to impersonal existence that goes beyond these perimeters.

This evolution from being self-centred to becoming universal is not easy. The strength and growth associated with this transformation demands commitment towards the higher and giving up the small in which there is no scope for passivity. As with success in any field, religion too demands sustained effort for very long. The quantum of success depends on the intensity of effort. At the lower end of the spectrum lies worldly prosperity and fame, while at the higher end lies acquisition of noble qualities like peace, compassion, charity, character, etc. The highest and the ultimate achievement for the religious is to become a world mover like Buddha, Jesus, Vivekananda, and others.

The range of this spectrum is best illustrated by a story about how Buddhism developed in Japan. A Buddhist monk wanted to convert people to the way of Buddha. The king of the land said let one minister practice it for a period, and if by the end of it he gained material prosperity, they would all accept the way. The monk then preached Buddhistic values to the minister, who indeed prospered within the stipulated period. As a consequence, people there adopted Buddhism.

This folklore may not be literally true, but it points at three stages of achievement effected by religion—prosperity (of the minister), nobility (of the monk), and pre-eminence of Buddha over everything else. The first two of these results—prosperity and nobility are the product of religious life, while the third one (when one becomes truly universal) comes through spirituality.

This may make one wonder if a person can prosper in the world by following the religious ways of life. Yes, one can, and does. There are two ways to prosper in the world—by fair practices, and by unfair means. Although it is often seen that people succeed by adopting unfair means, but not everyone takes to wrong means since people have the blueprint of goodness within them. To be a worshipper of unfair means, one would have had mastered it over births, something not done by all. So when it comes to adopting right means to lead one's life, one has to discipline the mind, since no one can ever be successful without mental discipline. This requires practice of ethical codes, of which the codes prescribed by religions are indeed the best. Marxists may preach that religion

15

is the opiate of the masses, but the fact is that religions are like mother's milk to noble minds. Ethics without religion can make one a gentleman, but religious ethics makes the practitioner a saint.

As described earlier, religion, and spirituality are intertwined. Religion takes care of one's existence in this world and the next through rituals, conducts, prayers, etc., while spirituality means to seek God, and God alone, without caring for existence in this world or the next. When spoken collectively, these two are called religion, and when one refers to only spirituality, it is called by its proper name.

The Uniqueness of Hinduism

Spirituality, i.e., giving up all for God, is neither possible nor required for a common man who loves his existence and wants his well being in this world, along with good times for his family and friends. For such persons religious practices, defined by the dos and don'ts, suffice.

And yet, there are always a few blessed ones in every society who find the world and its charms inane. It is they who bring gusts of freshness in the world by giving it an evolutionary push of an entirely different kind. Just imagine how life changed in Europe with the message of Christ, and how Buddha's message transformed life in Tibet.

A religion has to take care of both these types of people, and hence it has to preach the way to live a meaningful life in the world, and also has to reveal the way to get out of it. Every religion does this, but Hinduism specialises in preaching both the paths—life in the world (including heaven), and the way to get out of it. In fact, Hinduism is the only religion that preaches acquisition of wealth and enjoying pleasures as valid goals of life, as long as one does not make moral transgressions. These two aims in life are not considered to be the ultimate but are treated as important for people who have not yet come out of their desires, thus making it possible for anyone to accept the principles of Hinduism without any paradigm shift. And yet, ultimate freedom, characterised by complete renunciation, and total control over all mental functions leading to mukti, is the true goal of Hinduism.

These twin goals of Hinduism, prosperity and renunciation, make it unique.

It is popularly known that Buddhism stands for peace, Islam for brotherhood, Christianity for forgiveness, etc. In the same way, Hindu dharma stands for freedom and universal acceptance. Its goal is to make a person free at every level—physical, emotional, mental, and spiritual. Barring freedom in morality, there is no area of human activity where it does not encourage freedom, and thus tries to make everyone—men, women, children, elderly—free at all levels so that they can attain the final state of spiritual freedom, characterised by unlimited knowledge, wisdom, and strength.

Hinduism believes that not everyone is at the same stage of evolution, and hence people would require different paths to progress. So, paths leading to spiritual freedom is accepted to be unlimited, and hence it accepts every religion that helps one grow in knowledge and strength, leading to emotional and spiritual freedom, to be true. This acceptance is not like tolerating a neighbour or accepting his presence but is more like socialising freely with him and picking up his good qualities. This nature of Hindus made them accept Buddha as an incarnation of God, although he had opposed the principles of Hindu dharma in his lifetime. For the same reason many Hindus worship Jesus as God and celebrate Christmas much beyond eating cakes and lighting Christmas trees.

This basic nature to accept all makes Hinduism an inclusive religion. In comparison to this, every other religion is exclusive, which at times make them intolerant towards others. Only Hindu

Dharma accepts every past and future religion as a valid path to the Divine, and also treats each of them as its own. The sections that follow will reveal how every scripture of Hindu religion is based on the twin goals of freedom and universal acceptance.

Hinduism in Practice

Hinduism is based on the spiritual principles and realisations of the sages, which over the length of time got recorded in the books called the Vedas. Unlike other religions, it has no human founder, and hence its date of origin can never be fixed.

Although the term 'Hindu' is of relatively late origin, it has been accepted to signify the religion of the ethnic Indians and their spread wherever in the world. Hinduism is also the major religion of Nepal.

Hinduism does not claim any exclusive right over the spiritual truths it preaches, and it believes that a person can reach the spiritual goal through any path. This also makes it accept every faith and religion with respect. The history of India shows how it has been the shelter to the followers of every persecuted religion, and has also accommodated the proselytising ones, although Hinduism itself is not a proselytising religion.

Being an inclusive religion, it is difficult to define Hinduism the way Islam or Christianity can be. However, a Hindu is expected to have these core convictions:

• Acceptance of the spiritual truths as preached in the Vedas, and elaborated in any of the sacred books of the Hindus.

- The belief in the transmigratory nature of the individual soul till it attains mukti. This is the state of freedom from every kind of duality like birth and death, good and bad.
- Acceptance of different paths of religions as ways to perfection.

In matters of religious and social practices, Hindus go by what the elders of the society practise. However, all such practices are based on one or more of the innumerable sacred books of the Hindus. This section discusses in brief the foundation of Hindu religion, and its dynamics in the form of beliefs, rituals, customs, and worldview.

SCRIPTURES

The teachings of any religion consist of four facets: philosophy, mythologies, rituals, and ethics. Philosophy acts as the guiding light of spirituality; mythologies act as aid in understanding these philosophies; rituals are the concretised philosophy that one has to practise for one's spiritual upliftment; and ethics is about how one must conduct oneself in the world.

In every religion these four aspects are indistinguishably mixed in their sacred books. This makes it difficult to delink say, mythologies from spiritual facts. In Hinduism too these are mixed to some extent, but it also has four distinct classes of literature dedicated to each of these aspects. Each of these aspects has importance only if one wants to grow spiritually with its help.

Everything in Hinduism can be traced back to the Vedas. They contain spiritual truths, philosophy, devotion, mythology, rituals, code of conduct, ethics, poetry, etc. Sages and philosophers of later ages elaborated the ideas expressed in the Vedas to enrich various class of literature.

The philosophy comes mostly from the Upanishads and Gita; popular sacred texts like the *Ramayana–Mahabharata*–Purana literature provide religious guidance through stories and legends; Tantras–Puranas provide the rituals; and law books like *Manusmriti* provide the ethics for Hindus.

The religious and social practices of the Hindus keep changing with time, but the eternal spiritual principles, as recorded in the Vedas, continue to be the same. This dynamic equilibrium gives Hinduism an orthodox core, but a flexible external.

Vedas

The Vedas are the fountainhead of Hinduism. These sacred books are the most ancient preserved literature of the world, and it is difficult to say when exactly these works were composed.

According to educated guess, these are more than seven to 8,000 years old. The contents of these books are the records of the spiritual realisation of the sages of that period. Some of the mantras of the Vedas, including the Gaytri mantra are quite popular and are recited regularly by millions.

The Vedas are also called Shruti (lit. heard), since they were passed down from the teacher to the disciple orally and were considered too sacred to be written down. These are four in number: *Rig Veda, Sama Veda, Yajur Veda, Atharva Veda*. This division is based on poetic metres: *Rig Veda* is in *rik* metre (a particular Vedic metre), *Sama Veda* can be sung, *Yajur Veda* is in *yajus* metre (used as mantras during yajna), and *Atharva Veda* has composition both in prose and poetry.

Upanishads

The Upanishads are the last sections of the Vedas, but because of their special philosophical nature and importance, these are treated separately.

These books contain the philosophical truths realised by the sages, which now form the philosophical base of Hinduism. The most important of these truths is the Oneness of everything—*sarvam khalu idam Brahma*, and that the individual is one with the universal—*aham Brahma asmi*.

Ramayana and Mahabharata

Ramayana and *Mahabharata* are the two sacred epics that have served as the hope, ideal and inspiration of the Hindus. Of these, *Ramayana* centres the life of Sri Rama, while *Mahabharata* is woven around the story of Kaurava–Pandava clan in which Sri Krishna plays an important role.

Through narration, these sacred books highlight the struggle of an individual in holding on to religious principles in good times and also during crisis. In addition, these contain most other issues concerning religious life.

Many classics have been composed in every Indian and many South East Asian languages based on these two sacred epics.

Gita

The Gita is the most popular Hindu sacred book that can be treated as the handbook of Hinduism. Composed in mere 700 verses, it is a small part of the *Mahabharata*, but it stands in its own majesty of poetry, philosophy, and spirituality. Devout Hindus recite it daily as a source of inspiration, and also chant it when someone dies.

Puranas

The Puranas are 18 in number and form the mythological base of the Hindus. These have around 5.5 lakh verses through which the popular stories of gods and goddesses are described. The most popular of these books is *Srimad Bhagavata Purana* which deals mainly with the story of Sri Krishna. *Shiva Maha Purana* is another popular work centring Lord Shiva.

The Puranas were composed to suit the needs of the masses for an easy understanding of the spiritual truths. Despite their mythological nature, they discuss philosophy, ethics and rituals of the Hindus in detail.

Tantras

The Tantras are mostly about Mother worship through the ritualistic aspect of religion. Some of these books are devoted to Lord Shiva, and the rest are devoted to Shakti, the female principle of God. These books discuss ways and means to please Shakti, so that one can attain the desired in life. However, some of the practices of Tantra do not meet social approval, and hence these are not as popular as other sacred books.

Most Hindu rituals are derived either from the Puranas or from Tantra traditions.

In addition to these, there are thousands of books which serve as the basis for various *sampradaya* (religious sects) of the Hindus.

Smritis

The Smritis are the law books of the Hindus which prescribe the personal and social code. The rules laid down in these books cover practically everything—starting from the most trivial daily acts of an individual, through the duties of a king, to the highest philosophical wisdom that one may require to lead a good life. The aim of these books is to take a person to the highest spiritual realisation.

Unlike the codes of other religions, Smritis are not the dictates of God, or any divine personality, and hence they do not have the same veneration as the scriptures, or as the codes as practised in other religions. Sages like Manu took the more prevalent practices of the society and then gave them a religious orientation so that people identify themselves not only with goodness, but with religiosity too. The sages made sure to keep their respective Smritis in tune with the principles of the Vedas, even though these were written for a particular period of time.

There are innumerable Smritis of which the most famous is *Manusmriti*, written around the 2nd century BCE. The sages knew that a society ruled by archaic laws becomes stagnant. So, new Smritis were codified from time to time according to the need of the age. Unfortunately, no new Smriti of stature has been written in the last thousand years or so.

FUNDAMENTALS

The goal of a religion is to lead its follower towards that state of existence that is eternal and blissful, away from the dualities of the existence that we see around us. This can be achieved only through spiritual enlightenment, as revealed through the scriptures of that religion, and practised diligently by a follower for a long time till one attains enlightenment.

In essence, it requires the knowledge of the supreme reality (God), and other fundamental truth related to him, as also the ways and means to move towards him, away from the din of the senses.

Hinduism being a vast religion, the fundamentals discussed in the scriptures are much more than in other religions. This section discusses the nature of God, divinities, and sacred symbols essential for the spiritual growth for the follower of the Hindu path.

God

The essential difference between religion and every other branch of knowledge lie in religion's acceptance of non-material spiritual existence as the substratum of every material thing. The term used for this ultimate reality may differ from religion to religion, but its essential characteristics remain the same.

Since every religion is founded on the words of a master, the idea about God, etc. is usually uniform in most religions. Hinduism is different. Since many sages have contributed to its corpus, and they all agree that the infinite God cannot be expressed in a unique way, the ideas about God, divinities, and soul are plentiful. Here, only the main ideas are discussed.

The supreme reality in Hinduism is known as Sat-Chit-Ananda (Existence-Consciousness-Bliss), which carries two ideas—the impersonal, and the personal. The impersonal God is ever present and everywhere present for whom no adjective can be employed. He is infinite, ever free, without a form, and beyond the grasp of the human mind. This aspect of God is also known as *nirguna nirakara* Brahman (without any qualifying traits and form). This aspect of God can be experienced only in the highest non-dual state of meditation.

When this same reality is perceived through mind, keeping one's individuality intact but pure, It is known as *saguna sakara* Brahman (God with form and qualities, or simply God), who is merciful, powerful, and with innumerable noble qualities. He is the omnipresent creator, preserver, and destroyer of everything.

In essence, both these aspects of God are same, but people want to perceive them differently according to their mental makeup.

The personal aspect of God is worshipped by the Hindus in his different forms. Of these, Brahma is accepted as the creator, Vishnu as the sustainer, and Shiva as the destroyer of the universe, although in essence they are same. Vishnu is also known as Narayana, who is described as having incarnated many times in various forms. Two of his popular human incarnations are Rama and Krishna. The present day Hinduism worships mainly four forms of God: Vishnu, Shiva, Rama, and Krishna.

The creative principle of God is known as Shakti, the power of God. Also known as Mother, this aspect of God is worshipped variously as Durga, Kali, Lakshmi, and others. Independent of these, Saraswati is universally worshipped as the goddess of learning.

In addition to these, there are millions of gods and goddesses who represent the various aspects of divinity. According to some, there are in total 33 crore (330 million) of them, which allows a Hindu to choose a God of his liking.

Maya

Why and how God creates this universe, is a problem that has baffled philosophers since ancient times. For Hindus also, creation is a mystery of God that cannot be satisfactorily explained. After all, how can matter come out of consciousness?

Different Hindu philosophers offer different theories, but the most popular of them is the theory of maya, according to which, God creates the universe with the help of his own inscrutable maya (the great divine power), which by its very nature cannot be described.

Maya is the divine ignorance which exists both at individual and cosmic level. Maya is responsible for the wrong perception that people have regarding the presence or absence of a thing. Also, the continuance of the universe is due to maya; and time, space, events, name, and form are all products of maya.

Maya exists only till one does not realise the spiritual truth. Thus, it exists and yet it does not exist. It can be compared with the darkness of night that makes objects invisible, or makes them appear differently. When one wants to see this darkness with the help of the darkness, it cannot be seen; and when one wants to see it with the help of light, it vanishes. Just like that, maya cannot be comprehended through maya, and it ceases to exist when the divine light of knowledge dawns upon a person.

The existence of maya as real, unreal, or part real is accepted by most Hindu philosophers, but they differ about its exact nature. This gives rise to many schools of thoughts.

Avatara (Incarnation)

The idea of maya/shakti allows Hindus to accept the idea that God can and does incarnate in any form, including human beings, to give a push to spiritual evolution through his divine power. This inscrutable appearance of the infinite in the finite form is known as avatara. Unlike a common man's birth and acts, an avatara is not bound by the laws of the universe.

Whenever God incarnates, he gives the knowledge of spiritual path best suited for that age. It is then that people with devotional inclination feel the warmth of Lord's love, compassion, majesty, etc., and then turn towards him with intensity.

God would continue to incarnate till there is creation and created beings. That same God resides in every being as the essence, atman.

Atman

The supreme reality in Hinduism is known by various expressions. One of those expressions is Brahman, which alone exists—*Sarvam khalvidam Brahma.* The world and its objects are the divine play of name and form.

At the micro level, Brahman is known as atman, the conscious principle present in every living being. So, by its very nature atman can neither be created, nor destroyed. It has all powers, purity, omnipresence and is full of all knowledge. But due to maya, atman mistakenly identifies itself with the body, mind, and senses. It is then that it becomes transmigratory and is known as *jivatman*, which is equivalent to the popular idea of the soul.

The *jivatman* identifies itself with various kinds of action and their results, and thus goes on creating karma—good and bad. These karma cloud the pure nature of atman, and make him forgetful of its true nature, making it enjoy and suffer in the world. However, since the atman is infinite and eternal, it passes and evolves through various bodies and finally attains perfection and freedom.

Hinduism accepts that the true individuality of a person does not lie with his body or the mind, but with atman; and the real consciousness does not belong to the mind, but to the atman. It is the reflected consciousness of the atman in the mind (which serves like a mirror) that makes one perceive and know the objects of the world. When one's mind is cleansed through sadhana (spiritual practices), it serves as a perfect reflector of the spiritual reality.

The fundamental spiritual convictions and realisations related to God and soul, gave birth to various philosophies, worldview and practices.

Aum

Aum, in Sanskrit, is the universal sacred symbol of Hinduism. It is the nearest equivalent of God, and through its three letters of composition, A, U, M, signifies everything that is there in the universe. It is believed that *japam* (mental repetition) of this symbol, and a meditation on it can get a person everything that he wants in this world, and this can also take a person to the highest spiritual realisation. So, it is used extensively in mantras for recitation, worship, repetition, and meditation.

In addition to Aum, there are thousands of *beeja* (lit. seed) like *hrim, shrim, klim,* etc., that come from Tantra tradition. These *beeja* denote Mother power, and are used extensively in mantras and during worship.

DYNAMICS

The scriptures of a religion mostly contain spiritual truths that need to be applied to the society in such a way as to make these tangible to followers who are invariably at different levels of mental and spiritual evolution. The thinking minds need a rational approach, while lesser minds need rituals and customs that they can practise to feel themselves aligned with their religion.

Rituals, customs, and beliefs are necessarily of less importance compared to a religion's core spiritual truths. This opens them up for criticism and ridicule by the uninitiated, which is not fair. These (rituals, customs and beliefs) are the crystallised philosophy of any system—religious or social. It is through rituals, ceremonies, anniversaries and festivals that an individual remains tied with one's society. If these be taken away from any social group, it will be left with only the core principles that cannot be practised all the time, and hence the members would slowly wither away. Just imagine what would happen to school kids if there were not many celebrations and functions.

The goal of every ritual and custom in religion is to help a person hold on to something tangible, and then lead him slowly to the abstract. Rituals in religion are also like protective fences that help a sapling grow. And, like breaking down a fence to allow the plant grow into a full tree one has to outgrow rituals to become truly spiritual.

This section discusses the dynamics of Hindu religion that includes its philosophies, rituals, worldview, and the ways to mukti. It prescribes philosophy for the evolved minds, and advocates rituals and recitals for the less advanced. Its rituals are a combination of Puranic and Tantra traditions.

Philosophy

Philosophy is the science of knowledge, rooted in some subject, sacred books, or independent thinking. The ancient Greek philosophy is considered to be the most famous philosophy based on observation and inferences that influenced Christianity, rationality, and science.

The approach of Hindu philosophy (known as *darshan*) is completely different from this. Every Hindu philosophy is based on the Vedas, and in some cases on Tantra, and aim of each of these philosophies is to explain the material universe and spiritual reality through the words of these sacred books, since these are the records of the spiritual realisations of the sages.

Speculative philosophy, sophistry and independent thinking do not get much respect, since any of these systems can be outdone by a greater intellect.

The goal of every philosophy is to explain existence. Who I am? Wherefrom have I come? Where will I go once I die? Hindu philosophies address these questions in the light of the Vedic truths.

There are six Vedic philosophies based on the Vedas—Samkhya by Kapil, Yoga by Patanjali, Nyaya by Gautama, Vaiseshika by Kanada, Mimamsa by Jaimini, and Vedanta by Vyasa. Of these, Vedanta has three major and some minor schools of thoughts.

Over the period, Vedanta, in its three aspects, has come to be the chief philosophy of the Hindus. Vedanta means the essence of the Vedas, which implies that it focuses on finding out the spiritual essence of the Vedas. But since the Vedas are not the work of one person, there is no single outlook emerging out of it. Ultimately, three major approaches to Vedanta philosophy, Advaita, Dvaita, and Visishtadvaita, came up. These discuss the nature of God, soul and the universe.

According to Advaita *vedantins*, atman is identical with the supreme reality, Brahman; and the multiplicity that is seen everywhere is not real, but is imaginary due to maya.

For many other sages, atman is related to God in the same way as a leaf is connected with a tree. This view is called Visishtadvaita, which was popularised by Ramanujacharya.

According to some others, atman and God are two eternally separate beings and they have the relationship as between a servant and his master. This is called Dvaita, popularised by Madhvacharay.

These philosophies will be detailed in a later section. Other than these Vedic philosophies, there is the Charvaka philosophy of the materialists, and some schools based on Shiva and Shakti.

Aim of Hinduism

The ultimate goal of Hinduism is to lead a person towards mukti (freedom). But because not everyone is capable of taking up this great idea, Hinduism helps people improve their quality of life by offering three worldly ideals. Thus there are four of these, popularly known as *purusartha* (goals of life).

- Dharma, righteous living that results in a more meaningful life.
- Artha, acquisition of wealth through rightful means.
- Kama, enjoyment without transgressing the social and religious norms.
- Moksha, liberation from the cycle of birth and death.

The first of these three are for the householders, and the fourth one, spirituality, is for the *tyagi* (renunciates). It is expected that every Hindu would give up worldly attachments at some point of time to devote themselves fully to spirituality.

Worship

A common mind can identify itself with the great only through a concrete object. It is due to this that visiting sacred places and performing some form of worship or adoration is popular in every religion.

Hindus believe that God is present everywhere, and yet they worship anything that appeals to their mind. The object of worship ranges from rocks through trees to images. This sense of identifying God with external objects is not due to ignorance but due to a strong feeling of seeing the manifestation of the Divine even in objects and images. Ganesh, Vishnu, Shiva, Sun, and Durga are known as Pancha Devata and their worship is mandatory at the time of ritualistic worship.

Rituals

The most common ritual or puja is performed at home or at some temple in front of some image, idol, or some symbol like Shivalinga.The images and idols used during worship represent some aspects of the Divine. The practitioners either visualise the deities present within themselves, or try to feel their presence outside. In the external worship, the deities are usually worshipped with flowers, incense, and other offerings, or as the local practice may demand.

The truly religious and spiritual ones focus more on meditating on the Ishta Devata (the chosen ideal as taught by the spiritual teacher), and performing mental worship. The goal of every ritual in Hinduism is to ultimately lead a person towards the realisation that he is one with God. Unless one performs rituals with this idea, these are mere cages for the gullible.

Sects

Hinduism accepts inequality as a fact of existence. No two objects are identical, and no two minds can ever be same. So, the needs and aspirations of people can never be the same. Add to that a high number of sacred books, and a higher number of divinities, and the result would be a very high number of paths of spirituality. In fact, as many persons, so many paths, is the approach of Hinduism.

This results in a very high number of sects in Hinduism as compared to other religions. Each of these sects has its own spiritual ideal, scripture, and practices. However, the ideals and scriptures of all these sects are based on the spiritual truths of the Vedas only.

Purity

Although purity plays an important role in every religion, Hinduism appears pathological about it which makes it fussy about it in nearly every act of theirs. Sprinkling water, (particularly Ganga *jal*), washing, bathing, don't-touchism, caste inequalities, etc. are treated as matter of life and death.

The idea of purity flows from the core conviction that one cannot go near God unless completely pure, both internally and externally. In Hinduism, the higher ideal degenerated with time, making the religious appear obsessive about purity.

Festivals

There are thousands of festivals in India to celebrate various occasions. But unlike in other religions, Hinduism does not have a set of universally fixed festivals for all. Different festivals are important to different people depending on the sect or the region to which they belong. However, Holi (the festival of colours), and Diwali (the festival of lights) have universal appeal amongst the Hindus. Shivaratri, Sri Krishna Janmashtami, and Ramanavami are also treated as festival days by most Hindus.

There are also sacred days like Ekadashi (eleventh day of the lunar fortnight), lunar and solar eclipse, etc. on which special rituals are observed.

Food

Hindus have been quite fussy about the rightness of food over the ages, but the choice of food is local in nature. However, most Hindus (at least till now) avoid taking *uchhistha* (food already taken by someone).

Castes

Since ancient times, Hindu religion has been wrongly tagged with the caste system. Caste is essentially a socio-economic system which was taken up by religion to detail *svadharma* (the duties of a person) for a smooth spiritual journey. The goal was to take the lowest in the social hierarchy slowly towards the highest spiritual ideals. But the plot was lost somewhere. Today caste system stands as the great blunder of the Hindu society that chose to neglect its masses.

Custom

Hindus follow the rituals and customs of their locality and also what their ancestors and elders have followed. India being a vast land, and now the spread of Hinduism reaching all over the world, it is difficult to list the common customs. Doing namaskar with folded hands, and making pranams by touching the feet of the elders and the respected, are unique with the Hindus.

Creation

The desire to know how we came into being, and from where all this came, fascinates every thinking mind, although there is no clear answer to it, either from science or from religion. When one talks of 'singularity' in physics, and 'God's will' in religion to explain the beginning, one essentially talks of the unknowability of things beyond a point.

This idea of the inscrutability of creation is beautifully expressed in *Rig Veda* (X.129):

> *But, after all, who knows, and who can say*
> *Whence it all came, and how creation happened?*
> *The gods themselves are later than creation,*
> *So who knows truly whence it has arisen?*

Even though one cannot say for certain how the universe came into existence, one can make good guesses about it by inferring through one of the two approaches: bottom to up above, and, top to down below. In the bottom to up above approach, one analyses the effects and go looking for the more subtle cause, as science does. The other approach is taken up by religions that explain universe by what scriptures have to say about creation. It is of interest to know that no religion other than Hinduism discusses the bottom to up above theory of creation, as in the Yoga philosophy, which was later taken up by Vedanta.

Yoga relies on arriving at truth by oneself than to accepting theories and beliefs. In line with this, it shows how when a person starts meditating, he first mediates on some gross object, say, a flower. As the mind becomes concentrated, he tries to mediate on that flower without confining it in space-time. Once successful, he mediates on the subtler components of the flower. This is the point where Indian philosophy and the present-day physics part their ways. Physics tries to break down the flower into compounds, elements, molecules, atoms, and finally into subatomic particles.

But, the goal of Indian philosophy is not to explain the universe, but to realise God, so it does not care for the actual molecular structure of the flower, rather, it looks for the relevance of the flower to the observer, who takes it in through the five senses as touch, taste, colour, sound, and smell. Whatever the chemical composition of an object or its sub-atomic layout, ultimately the object will have to be observed by a person through the five senses that can grasp its specialised properties. The finer components of an object that are graspable by the senses are known as *tanmatras*, which are five in number for the five senses.

A yogi then learns to mediate on the constituent *tanmatras* of the flower, and slowly goes deeper into meditation when layers after layer of the covering that made the existence of flower possible, get uncovered. These layers are—matter, *tanmatras*, cosmic ego, cosmic intelligence, and unified existence. Beyond these rungs of the universe lies the spiritual reality that is variously called as atman, Purusha, God, etc. Practically no great Hindu sage ever contradicted this reverse flow of creation.

The top to down below models of creation in Hinduism too corroborate this process, described in its two hymns, *Purusha Suktam* (*RV*, X.90) and *Nasadiya Suktam* (*RV*, X.129). The first one takes up creation as having come out from, and by Purusha (God). The second one takes up the concept of the subtle becoming gross, and then acting on itself. It is thus that *prana* (the cosmic energy) hammers at *akasha* (The finest first particles) to produce gross matter, and the universe. Of these two, *Purusha Suktam* is nearer to the cosmological views of most religions in the world, while *Nasadiya Suktam* is nearer to the theories in modern physics.

Hinduism accepts both these theories, along with the reverse-cosmology of yoga, and harmonises them into a single, complete theory of creation. Accordingly, God alone existed in his formless aspect before creation. He is eternal, *sat* (real, because he exists) and also *asat* (because he is unknowable and indiscernible by the mind and senses). Since, he was indiscernible, there was only divine darkness before creation.

Desirous of creation, the Lord first created the three great elements (*sattva, rajas, tamas,* which are the mother particles for *tanmatras*) through his divine power, known as maya or shakti. This is the point when space-time duality is born. It is then that the Lord becomes knowable (only the spiritually evolved can do that), since his qualities through his creative powers now become evident. This is the personal God who is known variously as Narayana, Vishnu, etc., and it is this aspect of God that incarnates in the universe in various forms.

The first manifestation of creation is in the form of Brahma, the creator God who got down to his work as it was in the previous cycle of creation. Whatever qualities and emotions he assigned to different beings at the time of the first creation: good or bad, ferocity or gentleness, virtue or sin, truth or falsehood, that clung to them even afterwards. These qualities were in harmony with the respective qualities of the beings in the previous cycle. God and his creation are eternal in time and space, and hence, the question as to how these qualities arose first, does not make sense.

In the Hindu model of creation, God is not held directly responsible for it, or for the apparent disparity amongst beings. Also, creation is not treated as one-off affair; it has been going on indefinitely in cycles, and will continue to do so. These two aspects differentiate Hinduism from Semitic religions in a major way.

Sattva, Rajas, Tamas

When creation takes place from God, matter is not created from pure consciousness directly. The most important intermediary is known as maya or shakti, which is composed of three qualities—*sattva* (purity and stability), *rajas* (activity), *tamas* (inertia). These qualities always stay together.

When there is a perfect balance of these, there is no creation, but when it is time for creation, the balance is disturbed by the will of God. These qualities then get aggressive and try to overpower each other, and yet staying together all the while.

The entire universe and everything in it is driven by the forces and nature of these three qualities. It will be discussed in detail in the philosophy section.

Space

Like the theories of creation, there are innumerable ideas about cosmology that describe numerous worlds, planets and planes of existence (*loka*). The more popular view in Hindusim about it is that there are 14 *lokas* (planes of existence), of which seven are below and seven (including earth) above in which beings of different stature and mentality reside. The seven upper *lokas* are inhabited by beings who have spiritual light in varying degree, and the lower seven are inhabited by those who are less spiritually evolved. The residents of these planes have less freedom to perform new kind of action. The visible universe in which we live, is the plane of mixed existence where good and bad coexist, and one also has the freedom to perform new karma. Later the lower *lokas* were mixed up with the ideas of hell.

These *lokas* are not physical, but are at a subtler level of existence that can be seen only by yogis. These *lokas* are temporary abodes for life, and once the karma responsible for birth in these spheres is exhausted, the soul transmigrates to other forms and worlds of existence.

The idea of *lokas* evolved into concretised ideas about heaven and hell. Soon there were heavens dedicated to various Gods, and hells belonging to stern rulers. The devotees believe that to be in the heaven with their God is mukti, whereas Vedanta does not accept this.

The general idea is that heaven and hell are places of temporary residence where the soul (which takes up a body suitable for the place to enjoy or suffer) lands in its journey towards mukti— the final liberation from the law of karma. Since no one knows how these places look, the poets of the Puranas gave a free flight to their imagination to construct various heavens and hells, even though these do not have any significance in true spirituality.

Time

The Puranas have taken special care to define time. Starting from *nimesha* (time required to bat the eyelid), they go over to the life of Brahma, which is huge. This does not exactly tally with the time mechanism of present times, but most religious rites in India are still performed on this division of time.

The smallest perceptible unit of time is *nimesha*. 16,200 *nimesha* make one day-night. A human year is equal to one day-night of god, 360 years of men equals one year (*deva-varsha*) of gods. Through a long series of descriptions and calculations, Brahma's life span is calculated to be 30,91,73,76,00,00,000 human years. Indeed a long spell! When a new cycle begins, a new Brahma is born, who creates the universe as mentioned above.

These ideas about space and time must not be taken literally, since these had some practical purpose, as in the case of time division, but mostly these were meant to give a glimpse of what it might mean to be infinite, which God is. However, some interesting concepts do emerge from this cosmology and cosmogony (Time). The first one is the idea of cycle that plays a crucial role in Hindu mindset. According to this, there is nothing called a fresh creation—whatever is, has been earlier. The second one is that the micro and the macro have a similar pattern both in time and space. The third one is the idea of multiverse in which beings of different types reside. And, the fourth is the varying rate of flow of time in different universe of these multiverses. When it is one day for the gods, it has been a 100 years for the humans!

A person desirous of enjoying the world may go on doing so by getting born again and again on this earth or on any of the other planes. But there will always be some people who do not want to go through this meaningless appearance-disappearance cycle, and so they strive for freedom, which indeed is everyone's true nature.

Karma

The most profound doctrine of the Hindus is the law of karma, according to which 'one gets what one earns', and, what one thinks is as important as what one does in shaping one's future.

This law implies that the disparity in the world amongst people is not an act of God, but is due to one's own doing. One thus has the freedom to change one's situation by performing right action, and thinking right thoughts. So, ideas like destiny, predestination, and fate have no place in Hinduism. The grace of God, like the widespread rains, is everywhere, and one only has to make use of it through one's actions and thoughts to reap the benefit.

There is no historical point when the karma of an individual became operative; it is without beginning as maya and soul are. Like a flowing river, one may not know its source of origin, but one can go across it through spiritual practices.

Rebirth

One important fall out of the law of karma is the continuation of life in some form to work out one's karma. At the time of death, the individual atman (*jiva*) leaves the body, along with the mind to take up a new body. Depending on one's actions and attitude, one may be born in any of the visible or invisible forms, but the best way to work out one's karma is through a human body.

Transmigration is accepted in Hinduism, Buddhism, Jainism, and Sikhism. In contrast, the religions of West Asian origin do not accept this, and wonder why Indians are obsessed with this.

There are chiefly three reasons for accepting transmigration. The first one is that the theory of cause and effect (karma theory) does not become complete under a single life concept. One needs many births to reap the consequences, good or bad, of what one has performed by way of acts and intents.

The second reason is that the sages have repeatedly asserted this fact. Pure that they were in their intent, purpose and understanding, they had no reason to mislead people. These are the persons who gave up their all for the search of truth, so why should they be indulging in falsehood? Moreover, if any one sage had said something as a spiritual fact, as is done in most religions, one could have questioned that, but when many sages say the same thing, one has to accept it till its converse is proved.

The third reason is the innumerable cases of rebirth reported all over the world in which a child is known to remember his/her past life in graphic detail. Hindus accept such cases as a matter of fact, but do not like to discuss particular cases, since a person has made a new beginning with the new life. In the commendable work, *Where Reincarnation and Biology Intersect*, Ian Stevenson recorded innumerable such cases, but unfortunately the scientific community refused to acknowledge the work because of their own prejudices.

Beyond all these reasons and logic, there is the great principle of existence under the skin of this theory: it makes one accept the responsibility for one's situation. The experience of good or bad that comes to anyone is solely due to one's own doing, and no one else is responsible for it, not even God.

It follows from this that one can change one's future by working accordingly to that effect. This makes the theory of karma the most positive theory in the entire world of religions. It is a different matter that this theory is misinterpreted by the Hindus to be lazy and careless, blaming it on their karma.

The cycle of birth and death continues till one realises one's true nature as atman. This knowledge is popularly known as self-realisation. The ultimate goal of Hindu religion is to take every person to that state of knowledge when one realises his nature and goes beyond the cycle of birth and death.

Free Will

The law of karma implies that a person is free to choose the path that one takes, even though there would be impelling (not compelling) forces to make one go in some other direction. This idea of freedom appears to contradict the generally believed ideas about God's will, predestination, etc. So, how does Hinduism look at these contradictory issues?

Hindu scriptures and philosophy believe that the mind has intelligence, but it is not self-conscious, and hence it can never be free. The sense of freedom that people usually have, is a complete false idea—people do not even realise how they are dictated by their past. The true consciousness is only with the soul, and hence only the soul has the freedom to make a choice. Seen that way, one is fully free to make a choice, since the true individuality of a person lies with the soul. But the fact is that one identifies oneself only with the mind, and till one does that, one can never have the real freedom. Till then one will be forced to go by the tendencies acquired over births.

The spiritual cleansing, carried out through meditation, prayers, selfless acts, etc. make one free from body consciousness. It is then that one realises how God alone is the master, who controls everything as the indwelling spirit (*antaryamin*). Till one realises this, any theory about free will and predestination is as good or as bad as any other. For such people life goes on by jumping from one theory to the other and gathering experiences through that particular outlook in which one is then.

The Way

Every religion has two aspects: the higher and the practical. In its higher aspect, a religion takes one to God, and in its practical aspect it helps the votaries improve the quality of their life. Hinduism too does the same. In its practical aspect it shows how to improve one's quality of life. This is known as dharma, the way.

A religion defines the way in clear terms, and in many cases, it is defined in a straightjacket manner. Hinduism is different. There is no clear and defined way of life in it that everyone must follow. There is no unanimity about what are the practices that make one a Hindu. This confusion has been going in India since ages. 'What is the way?' was asked by a Yaksha (semi divine being) to Yudisthira in *Mahabharata*. The king said that there are too many scriptures, and innumerable sages, which make their instructions quite confusing. The true way lies hidden in the hearts of the individual, and hence the only way is to follow the greats.

Dharma, the way, in Hinduism, is thus strictly based on what the elders of a society followed, who usually follow one of the many Smritis (codes of conduct). Also, when a great person of a particular locality changes his way of life from the existing norm, people who follow him would change their practices too. It means that there can never be a single, unified code in Hindu religion. Hence, the idea of unity in diversity has been the core of Indian religion, philosophy, and the way of life.

Ethics

Hindu ethics is mostly elaborated in Smriti class of literature and deal with every possible issue that a person may come across in life. These codes of conduct are not based on what one sage said or did, but on the realistic ground of the ultimate spiritual truth of becoming all inclusive. The guiding principle behind these ethics and moral code is unselfishness. The goal of Indian spirituality is oneness, which implies that a person who is established in this knowledge, or wants to acquire this state, can never have emotions like jealousy, greed, ambition, hatred, etc., which are the signs of exclusiveness.

Sin

Sin, as a theological principle, does not play any role in Hinduism. The general term for it is *adharma*, to indulge in which implies transgression of certain code of conduct. Since these codes are not permanent in nature, transgressions can never be sin against God, as the term is generally understood. Sin is more like a mistake that can be corrected through penance and right action.

Sixteen Samskaras

The *samskaras* cover the entire gamut of a Hindu's life: from the moment he is conceived in the mother's womb, till his death. The Hindu sages realised that an artful life requires constant care, culture, and refinement, without which one would degenerate and become a savage. The transformation of the wild into the cultured is possible only through taming and training, which has been prescribed beautifully by the *samskaras* (sacraments) over thousands of years. All the *samskaras* and allied ceremonies are based on the philosophy that life is a progressive cycle through a series of incidents centering around the desire to live, to enjoy, to think, and to retire. It is with this idea that the rituals and sacrifices evolved, which were meant to sanctify one's life physically, emotionally, psychically, and spiritually. There are 16 *samskaras* that range from conception to funeral ceremonies.

1. Garbhadharana: The propitious day and time are fixed astrologically for *garbhadharana* (conception), and the ritual follows a set pattern.

2. Punsavanam: This ceremony is performed in the second, third and the fourth month of pregnancy.

3. Simantonnayana: This is performed during the period between the fifth and the eighth months of pregnancy. Its implications are that the pregnancy be fruitful, the child be endowed with sharp and penetrating intellect.

4. Jatakarma: This ceremony is performed before the umbilical cord of the child is severed. During the ceremony, the father looks at the face of the newly born infant, which at once redeems his debt to his ancestors.

5. Namakarana: The naming ceremony is performed normally on the tenth or twelfth day after birth. The practice of naming children after favourite deities began from the Puranic times. The rise of the Bhakti movement made this practice popular. By naming one's child after gods, one gets the opportunity of uttering God's name whenever the child's name is called out.

6. Niskramana: The infant is taken out of the house into the climate of fresh air and sunshine for the first time.

7. Annaprashana: This is the ceremony for the first feeding of cooked rice to the newborn. The object of this ceremony is to pray to gods with Vedic mantras to bless the child with good digestive powers, good thoughts and talents. It is performed when the child is six months old.

8. Chudakarma: This ceremony of the first tonsure is to be performed in the third year of the male child.

9. Karnavedha: The piercing of the child's ear should be done in the third or the fifth year from the date of birth.

10. Upanayana: The sacred thread ceremony entitled the child to study the Vedas and participate in Vedic functions. In essence, the child commenced his journey on the road to spiritual life only after this ceremony.

11. Samavartana: Upon completion of studies, the teacher used to hold a graduating ceremony in which instructions were given on how to lead the rest of life. Some of these are from Taittirya Upanishad.

   Speak the truth. Practise Dharma. Do not neglect the study of the Vedas. Do not swerve from the truth. Do not swerve from Dharma. Do not neglect (personal) welfare. Do not neglect prosperity (refers to righteous actions by which wealth is earned). Do not neglect the study and teaching of Vedas.

12. Vivaha: Marriage. In earlier times various modes of marriages were acceptable. Books like *Manusmriti* codify them, but in the present times, arranged marriages and consensual marriages alone are allowed. Acceptance of a child as one's own too could be through various means.

13. Grihastha ashrama: Entering the life of a householder. During this phase, a person was saddled with duties, some of which will be discussed in later sections.

14. Vanaprastha: A person was expected to give up his worldly responsibilities and privileges and go to the forest to lead a simple and solitary life.

15. Sannyasa: This is the last stage of a person's life in which a person renounces everything and devotes oneself exclusively to the contemplation of God.

16. Antyeshti: The last rites of the dead body, including cremation, are called the Antyeshti Samskara. There is no other Samskara thereafter for the body.

Of these 16, Hindus now perform only what they consider essential in their family traditions.

Five Daily Ritual

A very important part of the daily functions of the householder consists of a set of fivefold duties called Pancha Mahayajnas (five great sacrifices) through which a Hindu is expected to repay his debts to the sages, gods, ancestors, society, and the world that made one's life possible. Also, life is exclusive, but when one realises how life has been possible by the contributions of many, and then makes effort to repay the debts, one becomes inclusive.

- The first of these is Brahma yajna or the sacrifice in which one devotes time in meditation and study of sacred books.
- The second is Deva yajna, which is the ritualistic worship of gods and family deities.
- The third is Pitri yajna in which food is offered to the dead ancestors before one starts eating. This food is given away to birds.
- The fourth is Manushya yajna or the feeding of guests (*atithi*), giving daily alms to the poor, or doing some form of daily social service.
- The fifth one is Bhuta yajna in which one feeds animals and birds.

The Four Yogas

In Hinduism, religion is seen strictly as realisation of the Divine that takes one beyond the worldly emotions. Realisation comes in two aspects: the first one is from the texts of the Upanishads, according to which atman alone exists, which is one and same with Brahman, the supreme spiritual reality. The perception of the many, in spite of there being only one, is due to maya, which projects the one as many through the play of name and form, the way gold is seen as various ornaments. This approach is known as jnana.

The second approach to realisation comes mainly from the Puranas (whose spiritual essence are, in fact, non different from those of the Vedas and the Upanishads), according to which God alone exists. The world and its objects are merely the manifestations of God, who alone has become everything. This does not mean that everything is God (a popular mistake made by many), but it is the other way round—God is everything. An object is limited, so it can never be God. An image is not God, but God alone is manifested in the image. This approach is known as *bhakti* (devotion).

The innumerable spiritual ideals, as described in Hinduism, are variants of these two ideals only. One can attain one's ideal through any number of spiritual paths, which can be broadly classified into two—karma yoga (through action) and raja yoga (through meditation).

Any act of a person is known as karma (action). It means that even religious acts like worship, charity, service, prayer, puja, chants, japa, and meditation, etc. are karma. When these acts are performed with self-interest, one gets worldly prosperity and fame. But when these acts are performed without any self-interest, or as a service to God, then these purify the mind and make it fit for meditation and self-realisation. Every spiritual aspirant has to go through karma yoga for a long time before he becomes fit for meditation and spiritual life. Karma yoga burns down the wild growth of gross impurities of the mind.

In contrast, practice of meditation (yoga, or raja yoga) cleanses the mind free of the debris left by the burning down of weeds by karma yoga. It also destroys the subtle impurities that lurk in the crannies of the mind. The process of meditation has to be followed strictly as the teacher instructs his follower. The growth of an aspirant depends on the intensity of his practice.

Depending on the spiritual ideal of bhakti and jnana, described above, karma and yoga are practised broadly in two ways. The first one is when one directs the efforts towards God, and in the second one the effort is towards giving up everything, which is also known as *neti–neti* (not this, not this). This ideal, jnana, is practised by very few people, since it demands that one deny the reality of one's body and mind too, and hence this ideal is treated as the highest form of Vedanta. Indians, in general, practise various forms of bhakti, whose end result, in essence, is non-different from the knowledge aspect of Vedanta.

Samadhi

When the mind concentrates on a single thought for a long time, it stops taking in the impulses from the outside world. As the level of concentration increases, the power of mind increases, both for positive and negative objectives. Through proper training and control, the mind learns to stick to the goal, and keeps on becoming more concentrated, till that single thought of God, or the meaning of mantra alone remains in the mind. This state is known as samadhi.

In some cases, the mind goes a step beyond, and gives up that single thought (actually realisation) too. In that state, nothing else remains—the individual becomes one with the universal. But there is no way to describe that state, since mind does not function there, because of giving up even that single thought. This is known as *nirvikalpa samadhi*. This state is synonymous with self-knowledge, and mukti.

Mukti

The goal of every soul is freedom from bondage. The ignorance inherent in every mind about one's true nature (the eternally pure, conscious, and free atman), gives birth to identification with the non-eternal. This gives rise to desires to acquire the pleasurable, and run away from the unpleasant. This results in an individual's compulsion to act and work, which in turn causes more ignorance, more desires and more bondage. The cycle goes on.

The aim of Hinduism is to make a person conscious of this vicious cycle of ignorance-desire-action, which ultimately binds one to the law of karma and makes him suffer and enjoy variously. So, the spiritual practices in Hinduism are aimed at taking one beyond selfish action, and in making him absolutely unselfish. It is only then that one becomes fit for self-realisation, which leads to mukti.

Jivanmukti

The greatest contribution of Hinduism has been the idea that a person can attain the highest state of realisation and go beyond pleasure and pain, sorrow and hope, heaven and hell, good and bad even while living. In that state one realises oneself to be one with the supreme reality—*Aham Brahma Asmi*—'I am the Supreme Reality'. This is known as *jivanmukti*—free while alive.

If not for anything else, the Hindu race must be preserved and respected for possessing this highest spiritual truth. The echo of this truth has been heard many a times in other religions too, but it has never entered the mainstream of any other religious thought.

The discussion above gives a fair idea of what Hinduism truly stands for. Its derivatives at present, and also in future, can be unlimited, but their core is based, and will have to remain based on these principles only.

The scriptures alone are the true guide between right and wrong. So, lead your life according to what they prescribe.

— *(Gita, 16.24)*

SCRIPTURES

The Sacred Texts

VEDAS–UPANISHADS

Words are the persona of ideas. In its external form, a word is grasped by the senses, and in its internal form, it is grasped by the mind as idea.

Usually a person stays immersed in the ocean of words, absorbing and creating words, but there are occasions when a mind steers away from this din to enter the realm of silence. It is then that one comes up with profound ideas and sensitive expressions which take the form of living poetry, philosophy, art, science, and other branches of knowledge. These are the words born of silence.

In rare cases when a spiritual aspirant makes his mind pure by freeing itself of attachments, he goes deeper into stillness where his awareness of the world, words, ideas, and even mind itself stops. He then becomes intuitively aware of truths about the creator, creation, and the created.

The transcendental reality experienced in that stage is described to be beyond the grasp of speech and even beyond the comprehending powers of the mind. This may sound absurd, nevertheless it is true. God (call it by any name) is infinite (non-finite, to be more precise), as described by every scripture of the world. This infinity is different from the idea of infinity in physics, mathematics, or as commonly understood. Ordinarily, infinite implies hugeness like ocean or sky, largeness as with numbers, incomprehensibility or absurdity as in physics. But the infinity of God is different from all this, and has no imagery from our world to convey it, leaving the untrained bewildered as to its connotations. True spirituality lies in experiencing this infinite.

The Vedas belong to this category of transcendental spiritual truths, which have come down to us through an unbroken oral tradition of thousands of years.

VEDAS

The nature and character of the Vedas can be beautifully presented by a vision that Swami Vivekananda had on the banks of Indus in Punjab when he was travelling through the length and breadth of India in the 1880s. Talking about that vision, Swamiji was to say later, 'I saw an old man seated on the bank of the great river. Wave upon wave of darkness was rolling in upon him, and he was chanting from the *Rig Veda*:

Avahi varadé devi tyaksharé brahmavadini
Gaytri chandasam mata brahmayoni namo'stu té

O come! Thou effulgent one, thou bestower of blessings, signifier of Brahman in three letters! Salutation be to thee, O Gayatri, Mother of Vedic mantras, thou who hast sprung from Brahman!

He further described, 'Then I awoke and went on chanting. They were the tones that we used long ago...Shankaracharya had caught the rhythm of the Vedas, the national cadence. Indeed I always imagine that he had some vision such as mine when he was young, and recovered the ancient music that way. Anyway, his whole life's work is nothing but that, the throbbing of the beauty of the Vedas and Upanishads.' (*Complete Works of Swami Vivekananda*, Vol. IX).

This vision explains the origin, nature, form, and utility of the Vedas. The Vedic hymns are the prayers to various divinities; they were realised by the *rishi*s (sages) in the depths of their transcendental state; they are supposed to be handed down in a *guru-shishya parampara* (teacher-disciple tradition); they are the rhythm of the national life of India; and spiritual eminence can come to a person only when he catches the rhythm signified by the Vedas.

Origin

The term Veda, derived from *vid* (to know), denotes knowledge in totality, both discovered, and yet to be discovered. In a more particular sense, the Vedas mean the four Vedas, *Rig Veda, Sama Veda, Yajur Veda*, and *Atharva Veda*. These have not come down to us from a single personality, and hence Hinduism is treated as an impersonal religion without a founder. The way God is impersonal, Hinduism too is impersonal, and so are its scriptures.

The sages who came up with a particular hymn were not poets, but were the seers of the mantras, *rishi*s. The way Newton is the inventor of the law of gravitation that has been always in existence, these *rishi*s are the discoverers of spiritual truths. The name of the sage who came up with a particular mantra or a hymn, and the metre employed it are mentioned in every hymn. It is through this list that we know the names of sages like Angirasa, Kanva, Vasistha, Viswamitra, Agastya, etc. Later, these names became family names. This now makes it difficult to distinguish if a particular hymn belongs to a sage or to that family. In the tradition of sages, there were also *rishika* (female sages) like Maitreyi, Gargi, Lopamudra, Medha, and many others. There is also mention of child prodigies like Upamanyu, Satyakama, Aruni, and Nachiketa, who made their contributions to the Vedic corpus.

Till some time ago there was a ridiculous belief in India that females should not recite the Vedas, and not even the Gaytri mantra, which is the most sacred mantra for the Hindus. These self-appointed guardians of Hinduism forget that the Vedas have a good number of female sages who not only mastered the Vedas but also contributed to its body.

Vedic sages belong to an era about which history knows nothing, and from where only the faintest glimmer of tradition hints at the greatness of that forgotten past. No one knows for sure when the first sages started coming up with their realisations; some say it was 4,000 years ago, while others say it was a 1,00,000 years ago. But that is how the history of the forgotten people works. For our purpose, it is sufficient to know that the Vedas are the oldest available literature of the world. These sacred works were composed much before Rome was built, and long before the Greeks had started toying with the knowledge of physical sciences. What is truly awe inspiring about these voluminous scriptures is that they have come down to us through an oral tradition in exactly the way they were composed thousands of years ago.

To protect from loss, these were composed in certain poetic metres like Gaytri, and were then taught to worthy disciples in an oral tradition. The respect for the Vedas has been so deep that no later poet ever used those metres for their compositions. With the passage of time more and more hymns were added to the Vedic corpus, which made it difficult to manage them. There were also losses due to the dying away of some particular family before the family knowledge could be transferred. This required a radical move that was provided by Vyasa (?c. 2000 BCE), who was a great spiritual personage of his time. He collected all the available hymns from different traditions, and classified them into four groups.

The Vedic hymns are individually known as mantra, as opposed to shloka of later Sanskrit poetic works. Each of the mantras could be used, and are still used at three different levels—in sacrifices, as prayers, and for meditation. They produce results at physical, mental, and spiritual level respectively. For example, there is the famous Gaytri mantra recited everyday by millions of Hindus:

Aum bhur bhuvah svah tat savitur varenyam bhargo devasya dhimahi dhiyo yó nah pracodayat

We meditate on the effulgent Lord, who is the creator of the universe; who is worthy of worship, who is the embodiment of knowledge and light; may he enlighten our intellect.

It is used in sacrifices as a prayer to get riches; and is also used as a prayer to Sun God to wash away one's sins. However, its most popular use is for mediating on its meaning to attain spiritual enlightenment.

A collection of mantras in a particular prayer is known as *sukta*, or hymn. Vyasa compiled the *Rig Veda* by collecting the *rik* (pronounced ruik) mantras, which are a particular kind of chant, and are used as prayers during yajnas (sacrifices). The mantras of *Rig Veda* are known as *richa* (plural of *rik*).

Sama Veda is mostly a collection of mantras from the *Rig Veda* that can also be sung, and are used in certain special sacrifices. These are also known as *sama* songs. The *Yajur Veda* is composed of *yaju*s (prose mantras). These are used for pouring oblations in sacrifices. Most of its verses are taken from the *Rig Veda*, but it also contains some original prose mantras.

Whatever could not be grouped under these three Vedas, and were not required directly during a yajna, was put in *Atharva Veda*, which consists of a special class of Vedic texts known as *chhanda*. Apart from containing the spiritual truths, this Veda also deals with magic, spells, incantations, kingly duties, etc.

Vyasa gave the responsibility of preserving each of the four Vedas to four of his great disciples, of which Yajur Veda was with Vaishampaya, who had a prodigious disciple, Yajnavalkya. Due to some misunderstanding between the teacher and the disciple, Yajnavalkya was ordered to return all that he had learnt from the teacher. This infuriated Yajnavalkya, who vomited out all that he had learnt. Vaishampayana then asked his other disciples to take up the form of partridges and eat up the Vedic knowledge so that it could be preserved. The disciples did so. Yajnavalkya then left his guru and vowed not to have any human guru ever again. He sat down to perform intense *tapasya* of the Sun God, who taught him the *Yajur Veda* afresh. This version of *Yajur Veda* is called *Shukla Yajur Veda*. The original one, which was left with the disciples of Vaishampayan, came to be known as *Krishna Yajur Veda* because of the process involved in procuring the knowledge. Since then there are two different versions of *Yajur Veda*, although their content do not differ much.

The Vedas continued to be preserved through an oral tradition even after writing had become popular in India. Apparently, the Brahmins relied more on their prodigious memory than on the copying skills of someone. This gave the Vedas a special name, shruti (lit. that which should only be heard). These texts were treated so sacred and copying through writing was considered so unreliable that they were first written down sometime in the first millennium.

Even after the writing of the Vedas commenced, the oral tradition continued and is still prevalent. The early Vedic language had a pitch accent in which the same alphabet was used in three different ways: the higher on the musical scale, the normal, and the lower. In the scripts available now, the higher one is marked with a small upright stroke above a syllable, the lower one is marked with a horizontal line below the syllable, and the normal one is left unmarked.

The importance given to correct pronunciation and intonation of the Vedic mantras was so great that according to a popular story (*Taittiriya Samhita*, 2.4.12) Tvasta, the divine carpenter wanted to take revenge on Indra, the king of the gods. For this he performed a yajna to beget a son who would destroy Indra. When he chanted the mantra, '*Indrasatur varddhasva…*' he went wrong in intonation. He was supposed to pronounce 'Indra' without raising or lowering the syllables in it, whereas 'tru' and 'rddha' should have been raised. Had Tvasta intonated correctly, it would have meant 'May Tvasta's son grow to be the slayer of Indra'. Unfortunately, because of the wrong intonation, the mantra now meant, 'May Indra grow to be killer of this son (of mine).' Consequently, Tvasta's son was killed by Indra.

To maintain the absolute correctness of the Vedas, elaborate methodology were worked out. When, in the 19th century, Max Muller compiled the whole work for its first printing, the world was amazed to see that there was not a single alphabet's discrepancy between the manuscripts of any two families, though they lived separated by thousands of miles and had maintained them orally.

This meant that even the most ancient manuscripts were no more authentic than what the Brahmins of the period were reciting from memory. Marvelling at this unique feature of the Brahmins, Max Muller wrote in *India—What it can teach us?*

> I have had such students in my room at Oxford, who not only could repeat these hymns, but who repeated them with the proper accents (for Vedic Sanskrit has accents like Greek), nay who, when looking through my printed edition of the *Rig-Veda*, could point out a misprint without the slightest hesitation…a boy, who is to be brought up as a student of the *Rig-Veda*, has to spend about eight years in the house of his teacher. He has to learn ten books: first, the hymns of the *Rig-Veda*; then a prose treatise on sacrifices, called the Brahmana; then the so-called Forest-book or Aranyaks; then the rules of domestic ceremonies; and lastly, six treatises on pronunciation, grammar, etymology, metre, astronomy, and ceremonial. …These ten books, it has been calculated, contain nearly 30,000 lines, each line reckoned as thirty-two syllables.

A Few Hymns

Along with the growth and consolidation of the yajnas, prayer to the Divine also grew in importance. Importance of *yaju*s, the sacred mantras of *Yajur Veda*, pronounced in a low voice was believed to give results as derived in actual yajna. There were also declamations of verses, called shastras, in which 'Aum' was inserted at regular interval. References are also made in the Vedas to an 'internal' mental sacrifice that can be used in cases of urgency. The part played by thought, side by side with word and action is emphasised many times in various hymns. Later, this concept was taken up by various religious systems, and a devotee was advised to offer all his thinking, speaking, and action to the Lord.

These prayers, although used in yajna, have been used as variously as independent prayers, and also to convey the deep spiritual and philosophical urges of the Vedic, and consequently the Hindu people. As can be seen even in this extremely limited selection of verses, the sages perceived the infinite without putting a moratorium on its various aspects. This resulted in building up any number of relationships with him.

God, the source of power:

Who is the Deity we shall adore with our oblation?
He who bestows soul-force and vigour,
Whose law the whole world obeys, the cosmic powers obey,
Whose shadow is immortality and death. (RV, X.121.2)

God as lover, friend, guest, sage, etc.:

Draw thy friend to thee like a cow to milking:
O singer, wake up God the lover!
Move the hero for the gift of bounty
Like the vessel filled brimful with treasure. (RV, X.42.2)

We call on thee, lord of hosts,
The sage of sages, the most reputed of all;
The supreme king of spiritual knowledge, O Lord of spiritual wisdom!
Listen to us with thy graces, and sit in the place (of worship).
(RV, II.23.1)

Savita! God! send far away all evil; Send us what is good.
(RV, V.82.5)

Brahma among gods, the leader of poets,
The sage among the wise, the bull among wild animals,
The falcon amid vultures, the axe in the forest
Soma over the cleansing sieve goes singing. (RV, IX.96.6)

God, the one divine existence:

Millions are in Thy million, or
Thou art a billion in thyself. (AV, XIII.4)

Prayers from a full heart:

Had I been Thou,
Thy prayers should have their due fulfilment here. (RV, VIII.44.23)

As rats eat weavers' threads,
Cares are eating inside me, thy singer, O God Almighty!
Show Thy mercy on us at one, O Gracious Lord!
So, be like a father to us. (RV, X.33.3)

O God! I will not sell thee for the highest price,
Not for a thousand, nor for ten thousand, O mighty one,
Nor for an infinite amount, O Lord of countless wealth! (RV, VIII.1-5)

What is religion:

Truth, great law that is stern, consecration, austerity,
prayer and sacrifice, these uphold the earth.
May that Earth, the mistress of our past and future,
Make a wide world for us. (AV, XII.1.1)

Speech and silence:

Speech of four types has been measured;
The sages who are wise know them.
Three that are hidden in the cave (i.e. are mystic) are unutterable
Men speak the fourth. (RV, I.164.45)

The four types of speeches are known as *para, pashyanti, madhyama*
and *vaikhari.* Of these, *vaikhari,* is the uttered speech, *madhyama*
is the mental sound uttered during silence, *pashyanti* is the
spontaneous sound heard during depths of meditation by those

who pray a lot (of any religion), and *para* is the transcendental source of sound that produces the other three kinds of sounds, and consequently the languages.

One interesting hymn in the Vedas is *Devi Suktam* (*RV*, X.125) which is extensively used by Shakti worshippers all over India. Unlike in other poems, it narrates the prayer in the first person whose author is the female sage named Vak, and the deity of the hymn is also Vak, the Divine mother in the form of speech. The hymn shows how when one attains self-realisation, one identifies oneself with the universe, godhood, and the process of creation.

Sections of the Vedas

Other than these mantras and hymns, each Veda has three more sections: Brahmanas, Aranyakas, and Upanishads.

The Brahmanas are prose texts that discuss the technical details of the sacrifice. Every priest had to master it by memorising them and understanding how to apply them during a yajna.

The Aranyakas, or 'forest texts' are the concluding part of the Brahmanas that contain discussions on *upasana*, the meditation on sacrificial symbols. The Upanishads are the last section of the Vedas. Of these three, only the Upanishads continue to influence the lives and philosophy of the Hindus directly.

To perform a yajna one needed to know the Vedic hymns, and the science of performing it. In addition, one also needed to know the correct pronunciation (*siksha*), manual of rituals (*kalpa*), grammar (*vyakarana*), meaning of words used in the mantra (*nirukta*), knowledge of prosody (*chhanda*), and most importantly the knowledge of astronomy (*jyotisha*). These six branches known as Vedanga have given rise to the relevant branches of knowledge that are current even today in India.

The need for building altars for yajna resulted in development of skills that gave birth to geometry and later algebra. Later sage-mathematicians developed the idea of zero which is now the very basis of modern mathematics and the computers. Similarly, grammar, poetry, and astrology (not the predictive ones, which is occult) developed from the Vedangas.

Content

To the Vedic sages, the entire gamut of existence was a dynamic whole in which nothing was compartmentalised. Starting from an atom to the highest manifestation of God, everything had a place in which things evolved to find a new body and a new place in the tapestry of the wholeness of the universe. The difference between the lower and the higher existence, as between humans and gods, was not fundamental but was due to the difference in their manifested power, and so a lower being could reach a higher plane of existence through right kind of work or alternatively by knowing one's true nature. When people try to acquire power, they accept that it comes from outside; and when they believe that all power is dormant within them, they then try to acquire knowledge to unleash it.

Yajna in the Vedas

The Vedas suggested ways to do both—acquire power, and also unleash it. Those who believed in acquiring power from outside, adopted the ways of prayer and yajna; and those who believed in unleashing one's divine nature, took to meditation. The first types came to be known as ritualists, and the second ones came to be known as *vedantins*. However, the Vedas came to be identified more with rituals, gods, and yajna.

Yajna is performed by pouring oblations in the sacred fire to the Divine in anticipation of something in which the priest acts both as the agent of the sacrificer and the mouthpiece of the gods. Its antecedents lay in a very sublime hymn according to which even the act of creation by Purusha (God) was a yajna (*Purusa Sukta*, X.90) in which God himself was sacrificed to produce all that is there in the universe.

Over the period the sages came up with innumerable yajnas for different goals. It soon came to be accepted that one could acquire anything through yajna—one could get riches, find a noble wife, beget son, secure a place in heaven, destroy one's enemies, get rains, yield crops...everything through yajna. Soon there were prayers and chants for everything that a person wanted in this life or the next. There is even a prayer to de-addict a person from the vice of gambling (R*V*,X.34). The Brahmins boasted that they could even force the gods to come down through the proper performance of yajna. Viswamitra is supposed to have created a new heaven for his disciple through yajna.

One may find this idea of finding fulfilment to every want of life in yajna and prayers farfetched, but that is human nature. To ape is human. When Archimedes realised the principles of the lever, he is said to have proclaimed, 'Give me a place to stand and with a lever, I will move the whole world'. When Darwin came up with his theories, everything in life, literature and science was explained as evolutionary in nature. This also gave birth to the idea of superman in philosophy and literature discussed by the likes of Nietzsche and Bernard Shaw. When Einstein's Theory of Relativity became popular, it was lapped up by the society, and everything started getting defined as relative. Even morality and relationships were seen as relative. Freudians came to see the play of libido and mortido in everything—if a person liked something it was because of libido, and if he disliked it, then also it was due to the same libido! Now we have Marxists who see class struggle in everything. There is nothing in art, culture, society, religion, literature where they do not see class struggle. Limited as the human mind is, it wants to look for simple answers to put into pattern the complexities of life. The Vedas alone are not to be blamed for this.

However, the intent behind the yajna was different from what it was perceived to be. To impress the idea of divinity in the minds oozing with worldly desires, the teacher had to take them along the path of least resistance. To do this the sages popularised the concept of yajna (sacrifice), which served two purposes. A devout person engaged in yajna was forced to think of the Divine at least during the time of yajna, a thing which he would have never done otherwise. Secondly, that was the best way to bring a person out of the mire of his self-centredness, which is the opposite of spirituality. That was the only way to lead a person seething with passions like greed, anger, and jealousy, towards the plane of nobler thoughts.

Thus the true aim of the Vedas and their yajna was to make people detached, which is the true goal of Hindu religion. Heaven, pleasure, success, better life, and other such vanities of existence are not at all the ultimate goal of the Vedas, but detachment and unselfishness alone matter in them.

Gods in the Vedas

Oblivious to this grand intent, people continued their life centred on yajna, performed to please the innumerable Vedic gods of whom Indra, Mitra, Varun, Agni, Vayu were important. There were Vishnu and Rudra too, who became important divinities in later times. Mention is also there of goddesses, of whom, Usas and Sarasvati are the famous ones. There are also the wives of the gods, but they did not play any significant role in the religious life.

According to mythology, Aditi is the mother of twelve sons who are known as *aditya*s. Along with their companions, these *aditya*s came to be known as *deva*s (gods). The name comes from the Sanskrit root *da*, which signifies that they live in the heavens (*dyu loka*) as lighted beings (*deepan*), who are gracious (*daana*) to all creatures. In appearance and in their love for good things of life they are like human beings, but are markedly great and mighty. They regulate the order of nature, and conquer evil (*asura* and *dasa*). They hold sway over all beings, and no one can thwart their ordinances or live beyond the time they appoint. The fulfilment of desires of human beings depends on their satisfaction which can be achieved through offerings and prayers.

These traits of the gods made some scholars opine that the Vedic gods are like Greek gods in their nature and character. But a deeper study reveals that these gods are not definitive personalities, but are more like the masks of the infinite. The sages took up various aspects of nature, gave them a personality, meditated upon them, bared their principles and then tried to express the infinite through that. For example, Indra is described as having a body and is also described as being omnipresent and omnipotent. Most of these gods are treated as beings in whom the whole universe exists, who can read every mind, and who are also the rulers of the universe. This general principle of expressing the infinite differentiates the Vedic gods from the Greek gods, or the angels of the Abrahamic family of religions.

When the sages realised that the supreme reality could not be expressed satisfactorily through the existing masks, they discarded them and tried new ones, like Shiva and Vishnu, giving better principles behind their personalities. That is how these two became more popular in later days and continue to be so in our times. In some cases, the sages gave up the masks altogether, as in the case of formless Brahman in the Upanishads.

It was through this idea of infinity that the sages came up with the famous Vedic expression, *ekam sat vipra bahudha vadanti*— 'that which exists is One; sages call it by various names':

They call him Indra, Mitra, Varuna, Agni,
And there is the divine nobly winged Garutman
To what is One, sages give many a name
And call it Agni, Yama, Matarisvan. (RV, I.164.46)

This idea of unity in diversity has been the core of India religion, philosophy, and the way of life. What is known as 'acceptance' in Hinduism, actually flows from this fundamental fact of seeing the Divine as having myriads of masks, making it appear differently. Depending on one's mindset, a person prefers to perceive Divine in one or the other of these forms.

Monotheism (the doctrine of one and only one God) never found favours with the Vedic sages. The idea of sin and fear were felt to be demeaning, and the idea of 'the God' was felt to be inadequate to explain the world. When a Hindu claims that Krishna is God, he simultaneously accepts the divinity of say, Rama, Shiva, Vishnu, etc. This is the reason why Hinduism was never a proselytising religion, since it accepts God of other religions too to be true.

As in any early religion, the Vedas too have their share of evil. These are of two kinds. The higher and more powerful class are the aerial foes of the gods, known as the asuras. The mythologies tell us that sage Kashyap, one of the progenitors of all the living beings, had many wives. Aditi was one of them, who gave birth to the gods, while her own sisters, Diti and Danu gave birth to *daitya* and *danava*, who are collective called asuras. The gods and the asuras are thus stepbrothers.

Etymologically speaking, the asuras are those who depend on their brain and the brawn for strength, while the gods depend on the light of spiritual knowledge for their strength. Usually the power of physical energy is more, so the asuras regularly overpower the gods, who then have to get into various stratagems to regain what is rightfully theirs. Owing to their natural tendencies, the asuras end up being self-centred, while the gods have altruism as their chief characteristic.

Although Vedic wisdom appears to focus on yajna, their ancillaries, and their results in the form of worldly riches (*artha*), worldly pleasures (*kama*), and a secure life in heaven (*dharma*), the Vedas never lost the sight of spiritual eminence as the goal of life. The Vedas do talk a lot about acquiring this and that, but the undercurrent of the desire to know the Divine was always there. This bloomed fully in the Upanishads, and came to be seen as the fourth goal of life, moksha or mukti, which means ultimate freedom from the cycle of endless birth and death that is caused due to one's desires. One can attain this freedom by acquiring knowledge of the self, whose prerequisite is giving up of all worldly enjoyments. Thus, the four goals of life for a Hindu are *dharma, artha, kama, moksha*. The entire Indian religious literature discusses one or more of these goals. A book is termed shastra (scripture) if it discusses the ways, means and results of one of these aims of life. That is how Vatsyayana's treatise on enjoyment came to be known as *Kama Shastra*.

Thus the Vedas contain the religious and spiritual wisdom that a person needs to stay happy in this life, in the afterlife, and in the state that lie beyond both.

Creation and Universe

It was mentioned at the start of the chapter that words are the persona of ideas. In turn, objects are persona of respective words. Thus, ideas-words-objects are three facets of the same reality. The Hindu outlook is firm about this truth, and they thus believe that whatever is there in the universe has sprung from ideas whose Sanskrit word in early period was *shabda,* which now means word. Thus, the universe has sprung from the Vedas, since these are the ultimate repository of ideas. This may sound absurd, but it should be remembered that a word or an idea in the mind of a common person will not produce the respective object spontaneously, but the idea in the mind of God will produce objects effortlessly.

Once created, the universe runs on *ritam* (pronounced ruitam)—the world order. It implies the fundamental principles underlying creation and also permeating it. When it gets translated into the physical universe, it is the science of matter; when it gets translated into religious sacrifices, it becomes yajna; when it gets applied in social conduct, it is known as dharma; when it gets applied to speech, it is called truth, and likewise. The order in the universe is due to *ritam*. The planetary motion, laws of nature, change of seasons, day following night, flowering, crops, birth, death—everything is due to *ritam*.

This eternal correctness permeates the universe, but unlike God, it becomes violable in the world of duality and can be transgressed by the unwilling. The transgression is known as adharma (unrighteousness) which must be shunned by people who want to lead a religious life. Later, the idea of *ritam* evolved into the law of karma that ruled the individual's life, as also that of the universe.

Problem in Understanding the Vedas

The kind of Sanskrit used in the Vedas became obsolete long ago. The meaning of major portions of the *Rig Veda* can be made out, but some hymns and a great many mantras are quite obscure. In fact, the Vedas had started becoming difficult to understand as early as c. 700 BCE, as noted by Yaska, the author of the *Nirukta* (in which the Vedic grammar, etymology, and semantics are explained). A number of Vedic dictionaries had been composed much before the Christian era to explain the meanings of the words which were not current any more.

The second problem stems from a huge number of eulogies in the Vedas, known as Arthavada, to various sacrifices and gods. Since a common man cannot take to religion under normal conditions, the scriptures talk about gains to be made in this life and also in the next by the practice of religion. It is akin to cajoling children to make him eat or drink what is good for them. Unfortunately, immature minds take these inducements literally, and wrangle over it. Due to this, it is difficult to sieve the sugar of the spiritual truth from the sand of the Arthavada, in the Vedas, as in every other scripture of the world.

The third problem is rooted in the liberal use of religious myths in the Vedas. Myths play a very important role in everyone's life. But in religion they are not only important, they also become one of its four pillars, making it difficult to wean grain from the chaff unless taught by a true master.

Since the Vedas are not the work of one single person, and the organising principle by Vyasa was based strictly from the point of utility, it is meaningless to look for the evolution of spiritual ideas in it. These ideas are all mixed up, with the profound ones followed by some ordinary prayer. This makes a systematic understanding of the Vedas difficult. One either has to take up a few hymns for studying, or has to read the entire work with the help of commentaries to make sense of them.

Relevance in Present Times

A personality is shaped by the worldview one carries about him. A Hindu, living in any part of the world, knows that he is different from others because of the worldview in which he grew. This defining trait of a Hindu comes from the Vedas that have influenced the Hindu society, culture, language, ethics—everything —at a much deeper level than is apparent.

Although most Hindus never see Vedic texts in their lifetime, yet, anyone who claims to be a Hindu accepts the supreme authority of the Vedas in matters related to individual, social, philosophical, religious, and spiritual. When someone bows before Sri Rama, Krishna, Vishnu, Shiva, or Shakti, he unknowingly accepts the supremacy of the Vedas over everything else, since the very idea of godhood and its various manifestations comes directly from the Vedas.

The innumerable perceptions about God's nature, majesty, quality, appearance, and the relationship practised by the devoted were developed by the sages, who had taken up the fundamental ideas about the Divine from the Vedas, and then erected awesome structures of devotion to different divinities. For example, the ideas behind Sri Krishna's divine play, and Shiva's eternal dance are all rooted in the Vedas.

Whenever a sacred fire is lit, be it for marriage, funeral, sacred thread, puja or any other ritual, the mantras and the methodology is used directly from the Vedas. Similarly, the idea of acceptance by Hindus of the statement that all religions are true, comes from the Vedas.

Philosophies and sects that developed in the Indian subcontinent have taken differing positions on the Vedas. It was through this that India had the philosophies of Charvaka (materialism), Buddhism, and Jainism. Although these two religions, and also Sikhism do not accept the supremacy of the Vedas, they all accept Aum as sacred, transmigration of soul, and moksha as true.

The most important contribution of the Vedas is of course the Upanishads that continues to shape the philosophical, spiritual, and religious outlook of the Hindus.

One may wonder if the Vedas have any relevance in today's India. Isn't it enough that we are carrying their burden and repaying our debts to them by lighting the sacred fire once in a while? Why carry extra baggage when one has the option to travel light?

As discussed in this section, the aim of the Vedas is to help a person attain a higher life through yajna in its specific sense. The more liberal meaning of yajna, as described in the Gita and other later works is that yajna is the consecration of the mundane to the divine, the transformation of the profane into the sacred, the bridge between the material and the spiritual, and is the instrument to convert the belittled to the exalted. When an act is committed with a selfish motive, it ends up being mundane or profane. But when those very acts are performed with a religious outlook, they become yajna.

To lead a meaningful life, even while leading a worldly life, a person's every act has to be a yajna. His eating, drinking, sleeping, marriage, procreation—everything has to be a yajna, everything has to be divine. Those who do it consciously become blessed; those who do it unknowingly become peaceful; and those who live a life outside this become vulnerable to depression, suicides, intolerance, frustration, and other such negativities.

A gross mind may believe that it is enough to live a merry life and wait for death when all this will end for him in a single sweep, but the enlightened minds experienced (and not merely believed) the truth about existence to be different, and hence taught in one of the very sublime hymns:

> *vedahametam purusham mahantam adityavarnam tamasah parastat*
> *tamevam vidvan amrita iha bhavati nanyah pantha vidyateyanaya*
>
> I have known that great Purusha (supreme being) who is brilliant like the sun and who is beyond all darkness. One who knows him thus, becomes immortal (even) here. There is no other path for liberation than this (*Svetaswara Upanishad*).

This idea of ultimate freedom has been the national rhythm of India, which when caught by a person, makes him immortal. It is this message for which India stands today, and has stood from times much before Greek philosophy came into existence, or Roman empire was built. This message of freedom and acceptance from the Vedas was reverberating in India thousands of years before British people came out of their caves, or French people started becoming less tribal. Civilisations arose and faded, empires were built and destroyed, religious sects were formed and lost, only the divine tune of the Vedas continued to watch the impermanence from its stand of permanence.

The Vedas and their message are going to be around to watch many more appearances on the world stage and their exit.

THE UPANISHADS

The idea of the self, inherent and working within every life form, makes one live, love, and learn variously. In human beings, the crudest idea of self is seen in those whose life twirl around their body. For them, life begins with birth and ends with death, and hence they wish to claw from life as much as they can. Superior to them are those who identify themselves with their world of thought expressed in the form of art, literature, music, science, etc.

There are a rare few who outgrow their identity with their body, and also with the higher faculties of their mind to reach the state of divine oneness, characterised by universal love, unlimited existence, and unconditioned knowledge. In this state one becomes truly free—the liberated. He becomes a Buddha.

The Upanishads are the science of freedom through the knowledge of one's true self.

As mentioned in the earlier section, the Vedas show the way to a blessed life by consecrating one's actions, and they also reveal the science of freedom (mukti) from the world through spiritual efforts. In practice, however, the Vedas were identified with yajna that was believed to produce earthly and heavenly good. This was not to the liking of many whose spiritual urges were not to sate by the heavens and rebirths, which were after all an extension of present existence only. They wanted a more direct approach to spiritual wisdom, bereft of the paraphernalia associated with rituals. That need was fulfilled by the Upanishads.

Some historians see forces of rebellion (read, class struggle) against the Vedas in the rise and growth of the Upanishads. But the fact is that every overgrown system meets this kind of fate. Once a system loses its vitality by becoming less energy efficient, it is invariably replace by a more vibrant system. For example, one who wants to study Greek philosophy, Latin, Sanskrit, Western philosophy, modern physics, and some other subjects like this, have to study the respective subject in its entirety to first understand it, and then make use of it. Unless very much needed, people lose interest in such subjects because of their sheer size and so they prefer to go for a vibrant alternative. The same thing happens with a city, society, country, company, etc. when they overgrow. These get replaced by a better system, which too grows with time to be replaced by a new system. Thus the periodicity of overgrowth and replacement continues.

The Vedas too had the problem of excess. One had to spend the better part of one's life (around 32 years) mastering them! So the Upanishads replaced them as a direct approach to the Divine. With time the Upanishads too grew in large numbers, but as a system of knowledge these never became an overgrown system, since one does not have to read all the Upanishads to make use of them. If one knows any one Upanishad properly, he knows the essence of all the other Upanishads. This gives the Upanishads tremendous vitality, along with the age-old stability—something unusual in the history of human knowledge.

The last sections of each of the four Vedas are known as Upanishad. Since these come at the end of the Vedas, they are known as Vedanta. The term can also be interpreted to mean 'the essence of the Vedas'. The *vedantins* treat the Upanishads in this sense only. According to them, the rituals and other subject matter of the Vedas are the preparatory grounds for the final climb to the spiritual truths as presented in the Upanishads.

It is difficult to say how many Upanishads there are. The number is put anywhere between 108 and 1008. Acharya Shankara (c. 8th century), the great unifier of Hindu system of thought, has commented upon eleven principal Upanishads, and has referred to a few more in his commentaries. These Upanishads are respected more than others.

The Upanishads are not easy to understand without a commentary and a proper teacher. The truths presented in the Upanishads (these are not philosophical speculations) are so subtle and profound that only those with extremely sharp and penetrating minds can grasp them fully. To give an example, one of the smaller Upanishads is *Mandukya Upanishad* that has mere twelve mantras, which appear quite easy to understand. However, Gaudapada, the teacher's teacher of Shankaracharya, wrote an explanation (Karika) of it in around 250 verses, and then Shankaracharya wrote a commentary on the twelve mantras and the Karika to bring out its import. The entire book comes to a fairly good size, and is considered to be one of the essential but difficult works to understand Vedanta.

Content

Brahman: The Reality in the Upanishads

It was discussed in the section on the Vedas how sages perceived the Divine behind everything in the universe that gave rise to the idea of innumerable gods. Not satisfied with the multiplicity of the Divine, the sages went deeper and realised that there had to be only one reality. This gave rise to belief in one God, including ideas of sin and fear. This is known as monotheism. It accepts that there is One God who looks after the affairs of the world, while staying untouched by these. He is transcendent, but can be present in the world (according to some) without getting affected by anything. But this idea was soon given up, since it was considered too inadequate to explain the world. When science attacks religion, it is always on the idea of monotheism and its derivatives.

The sages then came to the realisation of the Divine as pure consciousness which was the reality beneath all existence. They called it Brahman (the Great) which had no qualifying traits, no attribute, no form, etc. This came to be known as *nirguna Brahman*, the impersonal God, who is ever present and everywhere present God for whom no adjective can be employed. The subject of discussion in every Upanishad is this.

Whatever is there in this universe, is Brahman. The diversity that one sees, comes from it, rests on it, and merges in it. The Upanishads use various examples for it—a spider and its web, or of a huge fire and its sparks. The whole and the part are in essence same, but appear different if perceived from different standpoints. He (or, it) is infinite, ever free, without a form, and beyond the grasp of the human mind. He cannot be called a knowing being, because knowledge belongs to the human mind; he cannot be called a reasoning being, because reasoning is a sign of weakness; he cannot be called a creating being, because none creates except in bondage.

The knowledge of Brahman is not like what one acquires about an object, or of the world. Knowledge implies observation, comparison and classification by the mind, but there is nothing in the physical or mental world with which Brahman can be compared. So the mind fails to comprehend Brahman. Highlighting this fundamental spiritual fact, the Upanishads repeatedly talk of Brahman as beyond the grasp of mind and speech.

In a conversation with Pandit Ishwarachandra Vidyasagar, Sri Ramakrishna (1836–1886) said that every word in this world had become *ucchistha* (tasted by the mouth), only Brhaman was still untouched. Pandit Vidyasagr was a great Sanskrit scholar, and so he could understand the implication of this statement. The highest reality of the Upanishads, Brahman, cannot be described in words, since the mind itself fails to grasp it.

So how does one know of its existence, since mind cannot grasp it? For the purpose of describing Brahman, the Upanishads employ the negation method, known as *neti-neti*—not this, not this:

'[*Turiya*] is not that which is conscious of the subjective [inner] world, nor that which is conscious of the objective [external] world, nor that which is conscious of both [between waking and dreaming], nor that is undifferentiated mass of consciousness [as in deep sleep]. It is not simple consciousness [in which one takes in the entire universe in one sweep, as God does], nor it is unconscious. It cannot be perceived [like an object], is unrelated [to anything in the world], incomprehensible [by the mind], non-inferable [through reasoning], non-imaginable, and indescribable. The essence of the Conscious manifesting as the idea of self, it is the cessation of all phenomena. It is all peace, all bliss, and non-dual.' (*Mandukya Upanishad* 7)

'Which otherwise cannot be seen or seized, which has no root or attributes, no eyes, no ears, no hands or feet.' (*Mundak Upanishad,* 1.1.6)

This kind of negation may make a person conclude that the ultimate state of reality is all void, as some schools of Buddhists came to believe. To negate that possibility, the Upanishads also describe its infinite nature as pervasive and with eyes, ears, hands, feet everywhere.

> 'Sitting he goes far, lying he goes everywhere; who else but men of purified and subtle understanding are qualified to know the God in whom all conflicting attributes meet? Without body, yet living in the body, untouched, yet seemingly in contact, omnipresent...'

Happiness lies in knowing Brahman, the Great—*yo vai bhuma tat sukham*. Brahman is not the object of knowledge but it is the eternal subject by whom everything is seen, heard, or observed. Since nothing can act on itself, the knower can never become the object of knowledge, even by the knower itself. So Brahman can never be the object of knowledge. No one can ever know it. Nor is it a subject the way one understands subject-object duality in the world. Since it alone exists, there is no object, and hence Brahman cannot be called a subject. So, the Upanishads describe Brahman as beyond subject-object duality. It is beyond good and bad, and virtue and vice.

Brahman is *sat* (existence), *chit* (consciousness), and *ananda* (bliss), since it exists, it is consciousness, and is full of bliss. Later Shankaracharya showed through subtle arguments how these three are not the qualities of Brahman, but these are its nature. He also showed how these three, although seemingly different, are one and same. So whether one calls the supreme reality as Brahman, or Sat, or Chit, or Ananda, or Satchitananda—these are all same.

To know this truth, one has to become one with it, 'The knower of Brahman becomes Brahman'. The triad of knower-knowledge-known disappears in that state, and what remains, remains. Only those who have experienced that state know its true nature. But even they cannot describe it for reasons described above.

When this reality is perceived through the mind, it appears as having qualities and attributes, and hence it is known as *saguna* Brahman (God with qualities). This is also known as God, who is merciful, powerful, and with innumerable noble qualities. He is the omnipresent creator, preserver, and destroyer of everything.

The Upanishads talk of both these aspects, but their speciality lies in discussing the impersonal aspect of Brahman.

Knowledge of Reality

The sages were so committed towards knowledge that they wanted to have the key by which one could acquire all knowledge. In answer to this question by a sage, it is said, 'Two kinds of knowledge must be known, the practical knowledge of the world, and the intuitive knowledge of the self by means of which the wise behold Brahman everywhere, which otherwise cannot be seen or felt, which has no root or attributes, no eyes or ears, no hands or feet; which is eternal and omnipresent, all-pervading.'

According to the sages, the world is important, and hence the knowledge to lead a meaningful life is important, but the key to all knowledge is the knowledge of Brahman. Whatever is in the universe, is Brahman, and hence by knowing it one knows everything, the way one knows the essence of all gold ornaments by knowing about gold.

The most accepted method of acquiring the knowledge of Brahman was to go to an accomplished teacher and get groomed into it. One meaning of the word 'Upanishads' is to sit near the teacher and master the science of self-knowledge. Alternatively, the word also means 'the knowledge that results in destroying the identifications of a person with the world'. So the Upanishads were always learnt directly from a teacher, and if not used as a technique of freedom, these were as meaningless as a heap of words.

Following this principle, nearly every Upanishad is in the form of a discourse by a teacher who was a renowned sage of the period. Even when a specific teacher is not mentioned, the presence of teacher is palpable in that Upanishad. Thus the authenticity of knowledge imparted by an Upanishad was maintained strictly at a personalised level. It is interesting to know that in spite of a large number of teachers mentioned in the Upanishads, their teachings are invariably the same.

However, grasping the truths of the Upanishads is not easy. One may go on hearing the sublime truths of the Upanishads all one's life, but they will not be able to grasp the truths unless the mind has been made ready. There is an amusing narration in which a teacher gives a difficult discourse on the subject matter of the Upanishads. At the end of the discourse the teacher is asked by his disciple to teach him Upanishad. To this the master replies that is what he had been doing till then! Well, if this is the plight of trained students of the period, one can only imagine how difficult it might be to grasp the truths of these works for minds that are attention-challenged, and thrive on e-information.

To acquire that knowledge (not mere information) one had to perform intense austerities, known as *tapasya*. The word comes from the root *tap* which means 'heat', and also knowledge. When one goes through the blazing heat of *tapasya* in the form of selfless service, devotion, meditation, scriptural studies, or any other austerities, all the dross of his mind burns up. The mind then becomes calm and fit to receive instructions. There are stories in the Upanishads in which a seeker goes to a teacher, and is asked to do *tapasya* for a period before his questions would be answered, and at times, would even be heard.

The calm minds could be stilled further. This state could reveal the reality directly. This is beautifully illustrated in the story of Satyakama, mentioned in *Chhandogya Upanishad*. He was an innocent child aspiring for knowledge. He was asked by his teacher to take his cows to the forest and come back when the herd numbered a thousand. Satyakama gladly accepted the task. The virtuous life, selfless service, and the ensuing stillness of the mind through these, made him a fit recipient of the knowledge. One day, he was approached by the bull of the herd, who informed him that they now numbered a thousand. The bull then instructed him in the knowledge of Brahman, adding that anyone who knows this and mediates on this shines in the world. To conclude, he added that the next set of teachings would come to him from Agni, the sacred fire.

Satyakama was then tutored successively in the supreme knowledge by Agni, a swan, and madgu (a diver-bird). Thus was completed the education of Satyakama by his four non-human teachers. When he reached the hermitage, his guru was surprised to see the shining face of Satyakama and so he queried about this. Satyakama narrated all that had happened, and added that since he did not have any human teacher, he wanted to hear the spiritual truths from him.

This story is indeed fascinating, for it shows how spiritual knowledge does not come from outside, but gushes forth at the mere external suggestion once the mind is free of emotions, as exemplified by the bull, fire, swan, and madgu. Another important thing worth noting is that Satyakama had already gained the supreme knowledge. His face shone with that knowledge, and even his own teacher certified him to be the knower of the self.

Atman

In the beginning it was mentioned how people have different ideas about their self. To differentiate these ideas, Hinduism came up with expressions like *dehatma* (body as self), *jivatma* (subtle body as self), atman (individual consciousness), and Brahman (the universal self). The Upanishads teach that atman is the true self of every individual, and that it is non-different from Brahman—the individual and the universal are same.

The general approach of the Upanishads is to lead a person from his gross ideas of self to the realisation of himself as the universal self. In one of the Upanishads, the teacher shows how his body, made by food, is his self. From there he leads the student to show vital forces working within his body as the self; then the mind as the self; intelligence as self; the 'I'ness appearing as the thin veil separating him from the universal self as his self; and finally atman as the true self, which is eternally conscious, beyond good and bad, virtue and vice, birth and death, etc.

In this state of non-dual existence, one realises that every idea of duality like pain and joy, good and bad, virtue and vice, birth and death, etc. was a mere illusion. Duality is ignorance; non-duality is knowledge. Wherever there is a sense of duality, one is afraid, one seeks, one suffers, but once a person knows that he alone exists, how can he ever be afraid of anyone, or seek anything, since there is no two? *Isa Upanishad* (6–7) describes this state:

'One who beholds all beings in the self, and the self in all beings, he cannot hate anyone. One who is established in the knowledge of oneness, how can he experience delusion, or sorrow?'

The ideas of weakness, fear, expectation, etc. are the products and play of the mind, and are never present in the true nature of a person, which is divine. The imagined incompleteness makes one desire, which in turn makes one work. Thus, the vicious cycle of ignorance (of one's true nature)–desire–action, continues forever, resulting in unending misery of grief and expectations. But once a person knows his true nature, he gets out of this cycle. He becomes free.

This spiritual knowledge is not speculative the way philosophy is, but it is intuitive. The technical word for it is non-indirect knowledge, which means that it is different from instinct, sensual, or inferential knowledge. Unlike every other kind of knowledge, spiritual knowledge is not acquired through the mind, but it is the consciousness itself that becomes conscious of its nature. The example used in Vedanta is that of a clear crystal in front of which a coloured flower is placed. The flower apparently influences the transparent nature of the crystal. But when the flower is removed, the crystal becomes what it was all along—clear. The true self of everyone is exactly like this crystal—free of any tinge.

In that state of knowledge one realises that his true identity is not with the body, mind, ego, or the complex of body-mind-ego, or any other such thing belonging to the perceivable world, but that it lies with pure consciousness that never alters its state, and is beyond happiness or misery. This truth has been famously summed up in a beautiful statement, '*Tat tvam asi*'—You are That.

Brihadarnayak Upanishad has the story of Yajnavalkya who had a conversation with his wife Maitreyi on the nature of atman. He said, '...It is not for the sake of the husband that the wife loves the husband, but for the sake of the atman that she loves the husband. (It is because she sees her own self in her husband). None loves the wife for the sake of the wife; but it is because one loves the self that one loves the wife. None loves the children for the children; but because one loves the self, therefore one loves the children. None loves wealth on account of the wealth; but because one loves the self, therefore one loves wealth...

This self is to be heard, reasoned about, and meditated upon. When that self has been heard, when that self has been seen, when that self has been realised, then alone all this becomes known…The atman cannot be understood or known, for it alone is the knower. Its nature cannot be said to be positively as such. it is realised through the method of negation of "not this, not this". The self is self-luminous, indestructible, unthinkable…

'The whole universe rises from him, and again goes down into him. No more is there any knowledge, dying or death… Where there are two, one sees another, one hears another, one welcomes another, one thinks of another, one knows another. But when everything is perceived as atman, who is then to be seen by whom, who is to be heard by whom, who is to be welcomed by whom, and who is to be known by whom?'

Kathopanishad narrates the popular story of Nachiketa who had been unfairly gifted to Yama, the God of virtue, and the overseer of afterlife. Yama allowed the boy to return, and also offered him three boons. The young boy's first request was that he be accepted by his father without any malice. His second request was to ask for the particulars of a yajna for going to the heaven, and as his third boon he wanted to know the secret of immortality. These three boons indicate how a person first wants his well-being in the world, and then wants to have a good life after death, and ultimately craves to know the secret of existence. It is only when a person's all worldly and heavenly desires are quenched that he begins the spiritual quest.

Yama fulfilled Nachiketa's first two wishes, but was not willing to unravel the mystery of atman to him. He tried to tempt the young boy into accepting various kinds of favours, but when the boy did not budge, Yama felt happy and said, 'There are two paths in life: one which appears good, the other which is actually good. He who takes the path of good becomes blessed, and he who takes up the road to enjoyment, becomes a degenerate.' Yama then went on to teach the young boy about the nature of self. The teachings came to be known as *Kathopanishad*, and it now forms a very important philosophical treatise on Vedanta.

Using the metaphor of a chariot, Yama taught that the body is like a chariot, the intellect like the charioteer, the mind is like the reins, the sense are like the horses, and the objects of the world are like the road on which the chariot is travelling. The traveller in the chariot is the atman that identifies itself with the body, the senses, and the mind. If the intellect (the controlling faculty of the mind) is always distracted, then the senses go wild, which ultimately brings ruin to the charioteer. So, one must strive to make one's determinative faculty strong so that the mind and senses remains under control. Yama further said that striving for spiritual knowledge is akin to walking on the sharp blade's edge. Even a little carelessness results in disaster.

In passing, it should be mentioned here that although atman is at times translated as soul for easy comprehension, the two terms are not interchangeable. The soul corresponds to the subtle body that transmigrates after death, goes to the heaven, etc., while atman is pure consciousness, beyond life and death.

Aum: Sound Equivalent of God

One important contribution of the Upanishads to Hinduism is the sacred sound symbol Aum.

In the Vedas section it was mentioned that there are four layers of sound of which the transcendental one is *para*. Those who practise deep meditation, hear this as an undulated sound resembling the sound of a deep gong. Sages have described this sound (*para*) as the last link of the meditator with the world before the mind merges in the Divine, and the first thing that the meditator becomes aware of when his mind returns from the state of the absolute to the world of relative. To know God one has to transcend this last link with the world that comes in the form of an unbroken sound, also known as the *anahat* (unbroken) or *pranav* (the sound of Aum). This sound being the ultimate link between the absolute and the relative, creation is also described as having come out of Word. The sages of the Upanishads named it Aum, which later came to be identified as the sound equivalent of God. The symbol is so expressive and universal that it was accepted by the Buddhists, Jains, and Sikhs too.

Aum is the symbolic representation of both personal and impersonal aspects of God, the way, say H denotes Hydrogen element in its entirety. When one looks at the created world, one realises that every object has three aspects: physical manifestation, verbal representation, and the idea behind the both. Thus every object in this world, seen and unseen, has a name that requires sound produced by the vocal system which begins with the guttural 'a', through velar 'u', and ending at the lips with 'm'. By combining these three sounds one gets 'Aum', which is the symbolic matrix of all sound, and hence the basis for all names. Since name and objects are non-different, and God being the matrix of all objects, 'Aum' is respected as the verbal representation of God. The silence that follows after one pronounces Aum, denotes the impersonal aspect of God, implying that it cannot have any attribute.

Hindus may squabble over many other things of their religion, but they all agree on the universality of Aum.

Vedanta

When a spiritual aspirant makes effort to gain knowledge, he first has to get rid of his desires for this life, and also afterlife. As one gains more and more spiritual knowledge through the calmness of his mind, one sees himself as atman, the conscious principle within him. This stage is known as *dvaita* (duality). If the aspirant continues with his spiritual practices, he comes to realise that the atman that is within him, is the essence of others too. This is known as *visishta advaita* (conditional non-dualism). Finally, the aspirant may come to realise that atman (what he took for his individual consciousness) alone exists, and that, it is non-different from Brahman, the ever existent reality, which is by its very nature pure, infinite, eternal, etc. This last state of self-knowledge is known as advaita.

Advaita is sometimes referred to as monism, but it is grossly incorrect. Monism implies presence of one, single entity, but Advaita is non-dual, implying that there are no two separate realities like consciousness and inertness, or mind and matter. Advaita implies that there is no way of knowing if it is one, or beyond the idea of one–two, since the mind itself ceases to exist in that state. The best way to describe the sate of Advaita is 'What is, is'; one cannot say anything else about it in defining terms.

The idea of Advaita, although quite incomprehensible by the common minds, is the highest realisation by the Hindu mind, and is its greatest contribution to the world of religions. This state has been compared to mixing pure water with pure water, and as realising oneself as the calm, majestic self instead of the volatile. There are other metaphors too. When a person realises his identity with the supreme Brahman, popularly known as *aham Brahma asmi* (I am Brahaman), one becomes free from the cycle of birth and death. Hinduism thus talks of achieving blessedness here and now, in this very life.

One who realises the truth that he is atman, is known as *jivanmukta*, free while living. This is the highest spiritual state that has ever been described in any religion, and is unique to Hinduism. This knowledge is undoubtedly the crown jewel of all spiritual knowledge. And, like any precious knowledge acquired by the human race, it has to preserved at any cost. If Hindu religion has a true distinctive feature, it is this knowledge of *jivanmukti*.

Relevance in Present Times

The Upanishads are the undiluted philosophy of Hinduism. Every other aspect of Hinduism follows the general principle of Vedanta—man is divine. In fact, every soul, every conscious form, and every particle is divine. The difference between any two life forms, or between inert matter and life form lies in the manifestation of that divinity. A conscious effort at it makes the manifestation more palpable.

As a thought system, and also as a way of life, the Upanishads are clearly the power, glory, and the ultimate achievement of the Hindu race. No other contribution by India to the world can ever match the majesty, sublimity, and vitality embodied in these sacred texts.

The revelations about God in the Upanishads resulted in the growth of two classes of spiritual paths in India—the path of knowledge (jnana), and the path of devotion (bhakti). The entire Hindu religion can be classified into these two categories. Of these, jnana is practised mostly by the monks, while bhakti is practised by all, even by most monks.

The Upanishads were not a Brahminical bastion, nor a male fief. One thus finds kings, Khshatriyas (warrior class), child prodigies, and female sages, endowed with this knowledge. In fact, no knowledge that claims to be universal can ever be exclusive to a class, gender, or religion. The universality and impersonal character of self-knowledge was utilised by sages like Buddha and saints like Kabir to make their life blessed.

In practice, however, the knowledge of the Upanishads was transmitted strictly through a teacher-disciple tradition, and so it came to be known as *sampradya vidya* (knowledge acquired through tradition). This caged the knowledge, and was at times utilised by the lucky souls to attain spiritual enlightenment. Swami Vivekananda changed it forever, and taught humanity to see the more practical aspect of Vedanta. If a person comes to believe that he in essence is atman, he would then believe that all knowledge and power is within him; and that he is beyond birth and death, and hence he would never be afraid of anything. By accepting and applying this simple truth, one can achieve anything in this world.

It has now become fashionable to talk about 'the power of positive thinking'. Essentially it talks about the power of the mind latent in a person, and indeed, those who make use of it are seen to improve their self-confidence. Similarly the fanatics believe that God is there for them, and that makes them do unimaginable, and even desperate acts. So, one can just imagine what the power of a person would be if he comes to believe that he is pure existence, beyond birth and death, manifesting as everyone and everything else! He would go beyond fears, and he would also become compassionate.

Hindus may someday give up its tryst with materialism; it may give up its idols, gods and goddesses; and, it may even give up its God; but it will never give up the truth that 'man is divine', nor will it stop spreading this message to the world.

This is Practical Vedanta, and this is going to be the future philosophy and way of life for the Hindu race if it has to survive, and be the best in the world.

Popular Scriptures

ITIHASA–PURANA

When Einstein first came up with the Theory of Relativity, it is said that only a handful of scientists could understand it. It then took decades and scores of brilliant minds to work out the practical aspects of the theory that resulted in the knowledge of nuclear energy, big bang, black holes, the expanding universe and other such. And it took a 100 years for the scientists to verify the existence of gravitational waves that had been predicted by the great scientist. One can thus see how it is one thing to come up with a grand scientific truth, and it is another to work out its implications. What to say then of making it comprehensible to non-technical minds!

This holds true for religions too. A sage may have revelation, but to make it comprehensible to the common mind is never easy. It is due to this that even though the Vedas are profound, eternal, impersonal, and universal, these can be grasped and used by trained spiritual minds only.

The two limitations of incomprehensibility and specialised practicability created yawning chasms between the spirituality of the Vedas and the spiritual urges of the Hindu society. The conduit between them was erected by Valmiki and Vyasa, the two great sage poets, through their creation of Itihasa–Purana literature. These sacred books took the help of stories, myths, legends, history, etc. to make sublime truths accessible to all, irrespective of their caste or gender. It was like converting the pure solar energy through photosynthesis into vegetation that can be used as food by living beings.

Stories and myths are used to explain concepts that cannot be satisfactorily expressed through words. Usually ideas ride on crests of words, but some ideas are too subtle to travel directly on them, and so they require a lot of supportive gears before they can be transmitted. The spiritual truths of the Vedas and the Upanishads belong to this category, and hence stories and myths are needed to be expressed in words to make them comprehensible to the non-specialised minds.

Religious myths of the Hindus, known as Puranas, meaning 'old stories that are ever fresh', were current in India from the Vedic times, or maybe even earlier. The great sage Vyasa is believed to have collected and written them down cohesively. Later sages added to the corpus and passed them off in the name of Vyasa to gain credence. This resulted in 18 huge volumes of Puranas (and 18 equally large Upa-Puranas) that describe awe inspiring stories centring the Divine. Their nature and character will be discussed a little later.

Valmiki's *Ramayana* and Vyasa's *Mahabharata* are known as Itihasa (lit. history). Unlike the present idea of history in which events are described as these happened (or as the historians want them to be seen), Itihasa were not the history of kings, queens, wars, and exploits far removed in time and land. This kind of history can sate one's curiosity, but when it comes to contributing to the culture of a race, it is just rubbish. For a Hindu, the meaning and purpose of life centres on the individual, and hence all that one does has to centre on one's growth.

For example, how does it matter to a devotee whether Buddha was born 2500 years ago, or 3500 years ago? Or whether the names of his parents were this or that? When it comes to one's growth, it is only Buddha's life and message that act as spiritual nourishment. Indian sages realised this fact and so they used events and personalities of bygone era to create scriptures through which one could make one's life blessed. Itihasa are thus neither the history of the Indian race, nor pieces of literature, but are the historical record of its hopes, aspirations, urges, understanding, and spiritual evolution.

These (*Ramayana* and *Mahabharata*) are epical in composition, woven around human personalities. In addition to stories and legends, these also contain prayers as in the Vedas, philosophy as in the Upanishads, and stories as in the Puranas. Itihasa are thus like the midway house between the real of the Upanishads and the myths of the Puranas.

Itihasa–Purana are not mere epics, but scriptures. Scriptures are defined as sacred works that lead a person to attain one of the four goals of life—*artha* (wealth), *kama* (enjoyment in the world), *dharma* (noble acts), and *moksha* (liberation from the cycle of birth and death).

Since Itihasa–Purana discuss in detail ways to attain these goals, and their spiritual message being the same as in the Vedas, these are treated nearly at par with the Vedas, but to differentiate them, the Vedas are known as Shruti, and these works are known as Smriti. According to a popular verse, the knowledge of Itihasa–Purana is essential to understand the Vedas.

The relation between the Vedas and Itihasa–Purana can be best described as between soul and body. The soul requires a body to express its aspirations, excellence, and majesty, even though a body is insignificant before it. The body being more visible and comprehensible, people usually attach themselves with it only. Even in the world hardly anyone loves others for his soul, or even the mind—everyone ends up loving only the body. Even a mom loves her baby only through the body; she does not even care to understand the inner nature of her child.

The Vedas are the soul of Hinduism, while Itihasa–Purana are its body. Gross as our minds are, we cannot appreciate the soul directly, and hence we have to look at its expression through the body only. Only a few evolved minds can look beyond the body to have a peep at the ideas that they represent. This example may appear crude nevertheless it conveys the idea.

With time, Itihasa–Purana came to be the mainframe of Hinduism due to various reasons that will be discussed in this section. Hindus of present times usually treat any one or more of these popular scriptures as the guiding book of their social, moral, religious, and spiritual life. It is a different matter that in most cases people hardly take the spiritual message of these sacred books, and only fantasise over the mythical.

Ramayana and *Mahabharata* also made a deep impact on the literary landscape of India. Many classics have been composed in most of the Indian and many Southeast Asian languages based on these two sacred epics. Of these, *Ramayana* centres the life of Sri Rama, while *Mahabharata* is woven around the story of the Kaurava–Pandava clan in which Sri Krishna plays an important role. These sacred books highlight the struggle of an individual in holding on to religious principles in good times and also during crisis. In addition, these contain most other issues concerning religious life.

RAMAYANA

It has been a common practice in India to greet others with 'Rama Rama'; count and weigh things as 'Rama'; approve a thing by saying 'Rama'; disapprove something by saying 'Rama Rama', chant 'Rama' during funeral; marry off young couples through Rama-Sita traditions; and die with the name of Rama on lips, the way Gandhiji did.

The spiritually indifferent Hindus may not know much of these practices, but even they love watching *Ramayana* serial (for war scenes), and go to watch the burning of Ravana on Dussehra (for *tamasha*) year after year. Every Hindu grows up on a liberal intake of *Ramayana* in different formats like serials, cartoons, story books, *Amar Chitra Katha* series, etc., and people flock to watch Ram Leela, year after year, even though they know every inch of the story since their childhood. In 1980s when *Ramayana*, the serial, was being telecast, practically the entire nation used to come to a standstill during that one hour!

This shows how *Ramayana* is not a mere epic but a spiritual work. A book is read, reread, and narrated repeatedly only when it can slake the spiritual thirst of people, even though they may not be aware of it. A newborn does not know that he is hungry, but his inner urges make him crave and cry for food. Something similar happens with the spiritual hunger of people. They strive to quench their urges instinctively through spiritual stories till they evolve to be able to grasp the message behind them.

It is worth mentioning here that the *Iliad* and the *Odyssey*, the two famous Greek epics, were essentially religious works that were sung and recited in every home till Homer made epics out of them. From the time that the spiritual elements were taken away from the story by Homer, the tradition of reciting and narrating them slowly died away. In Indian tradition also, two great works by Kalidasa, *Raghuvamsam* and *Kumarasambhavam* are stories based on Sri Rama and Lord Shiva. However, these books are confined to the academic world, while *Ramayana* and the Puranas are recited regularly all over the country.

The story goes that when Valmiki got down to composing *Ramayana*, he was blessed by Brahma: 'The theme of *Ramayana* will remain popular in the world so long as mountains and rivers will remain on the surfaces of the earth.' This came to be true literally, and later poets took up the story of Sri Rama to create different versions of the *Ramayana* in Sanskrit and every Indian language that has made it a household narrative all over India, and is treated as a popular legend in South and South Asian countries. These narrations do differ in detail, since these were written to cater to mindsets of different land and times, but these are all based on the story of Rama in *Ramayana* by Valmiki, who composed it thousands of years ago in 24,000 shlokas (verses) arranged in 6 sections.

Content

The personalised presentation of spirituality in the *Ramayana* makes it easy to relate as it is both appealing and practical. In addition, Valmiki had an excellent grasp over the Indian religious ethos, which he put to great use by spraying it liberally in the story to make it a storehouse of religious wisdom, philosophy, values, and practices. It was through these that *Ramayana* became the great influence in India, and defined aspects of religion that shaped modern Hinduism.

The story of Sri Rama is too popular to need narration and hence only certain aspects of religion and ethics that have come to be the mainstay of Hinduism will be discussed here.

Role of Yajna and Tapasya

Valmiki was a sage of Vedic times when Vedic wisdom, gods, yajna, and sages were revered in all their glory. Rama is thus described as having been born through the performance of yajna by his parents in which the gods came to accept the offering, and Vishnu, a Vedic god, promised to take up the body of Rama to destroy Ravana who was terrorising the world through his acts.

Valmiki lent importance to yajna, and also stressed on the need for spiritual austerities in the form of *tapasya* to attain spiritual eminence, and also as a way of life. *Tapasya* is like building one's storehouse of energy to surmount the problems that arise due to various external and internal factors. Like creating a dam to increase the volume of water, *tapasya* stores the psychic energy. *Ramayana* mentions many sages who had chosen *tapasya* as a way of life. The Upanishads do talk about sages doing *tapasya*, but Valmiki had people from all walks of life performing *tapasya* for various reasons, including penance.

Idea of a Divine Superhero

The concept of the incarnation of God had not yet evolved during the times of Valmiki, so he treats Sri Rama as a divine superhero. It was left for later sages and poets to transform the divinely heroic personality of Rama into that of God. Sacred books in Sanskrit like *Adhyatma Ramayana*, and *Ramacharitmanas* in Hindi by Tulasidas are good examples of this devotional approach. India being a land of religion, this approach became much more popular than what Valmiki had offered.

One may wonder if this transference of godhood onto a personality is fair. The fact is that India or any other land never worships personalities, but worships only the ideas centring in

God. It was mentioned in the section on the Vedas how Indra and other gods were taken up to represent the infinite, but were found wanting due to various reasons. The personality of Rama, and later Sri Krishna, were felt to be better masks of the infinite through which a devotee could feel the presence and compassion of God.

Rama is portrayed as superhuman through his holding on to his duties even during adversity. But in a more interesting episode, Rama is seen to get furious with the Ocean God because there was no way to cross it to reach Lanka, the land of Ravana, to liberate Sita. So Rama picks up his divine arrows to dry up the ocean to get passage. The Ocean God comes before Rama and firmly replies that he could not give up his dharma for fear or greed, and hence he would not part himself to give way to Rama's army. However, Rama could make a bridge through the ocean, he suggested.

Temptation and Redemption

The problem of temptation, its consequences, and redemption from it are found at regular intervals in *Ramayana*. There was a great sage Rishyasringa, who was born out of the temptation of his sage-father, and he himself was lured away by dancing girls to be married off to a princess. In spite of all this, Rishyasringa continued to be a great sage, who was invited to perform the yajna by which Sri Rama was born. In contrast to this there is the innocent temptation of Sita for the golden deer that resulted in her getting kidnapped, and consequently the war that resulted in the neutralisation of Ravana and his clan.

The way to redemption from temptations is *tapasya*, in which a person gives up bodily desires and needs to focus on the Divine. This brings back the glory of the soul and subdues the eminence of the body. The idea of sin, as commonly understood, does not find a place in the *Ramayana*, nor in Hinduism. Sin is a transgression of moral code acquired through sacred books and words of elders. There being no sin against God, no one can ever be condemned eternally, and hence every transgression can be corrected through *tapasya*. For example, when Ahalya, wife of the great sage Gautam, committed moral transgressions, she was asked by the infuriated sage to perform *tapasya* to purify herself. She devoted herself to *tapasya* for a long time and became the sage-wife once again.

This kind of *tapasya* makes one's mind free of selfish motives, and thus makes it fit to be the ultimate judge in matters of guilt and transgressions. When Mahavir Hanuman entered the palace of Ravana at night in search of Sita, he went around the palace looking at the hundreds of wives of Ravana, who were fast asleep in various postures. When he had seen them all and concluded that Sita could not be there, he got worried about his own moral transgression. He felt that he had committed gross immorality by looking at those women in their inner chambers while they were sleeping and were not careful about themselves. He got scared that this might destroy all his dharma. But he then realised that he had not looked at them with any passion, and that his mind and senses had not been disturbed even a little when he was looking at them. This calmed him down. He concluded that since mind alone was responsible for a person's good or bad action, and since his mind had not undergone any disturbance, so there had been no moral lapse on his part.

Living in the Moment

Ramayana lays emphasis on the present life much more than the next life, and encouraged equal emphasis on *dharma*, *artha*, and *kama*. When Rama went into the exile, Bharata, his younger brother became the king. He was unaware of the politics behind Rama's expulsion, so he went to the forest in search of Rama to request him to return, Rama refused to do so, but advised Bharata how to lead a balanced life in matters of pleasures, acquisition, and religious pursuits. A person was expected not to pay excessive attention to one of these over the other. Later sages, of course, brought in the idea of moksha as the primary moving force in spiritual life.

Role of Goodness

Ramayana is the story woven around various aspects of goodness as spiritual value. It describes what it means to be a good son, brother, wife, husband, king, subordinate, friend, and even a good enemy through the various characters spread around the central personality of Sri Rama. In the process, it deals with different obstacles faced in practising goodness. This sacred book is thus like a spiritual mirror in which one can see reflections of one's spiritual personality, growth, and also the end result of this growth (or lack of it).

According to Hinduism, life is not a journey from being bad to good, but it is the struggle from being good to better. The desire to be good and to be seen as good is inherent in human beings. Even skewed characters crave to be seen as good by their loved ones. This is so because goodness is God, and being divine, it is in the nature of human beings to be good.

When a person is good only towards a limited circle of people, his goodness is treated as ordinary, but when his goodness encompasses a larger circle, he is respected as noble. A good person may not be spiritual since his goodness may be due to social forces, but a spiritual person is necessarily good, since spirituality always works from within.

But as is well known, it is difficult to be good, and it is much more difficult to trudge the path of goodness. Try howsoever, he who opts to take the path of good invariably finds it slippery, tortuous and full of obstacles that results in pain and even ignominy. It is well known how Socrates had to face untimely death simply because he refused to give up the path of truth. This, of course, does not mean that one can take the easy path out, for the travellers of path of unrighteousness not only meet their doom, but also bring ruin to all those who have a connection with them.

The usual obstacles on the path of goodness are fear and temptation. It is because goodness is the nature of the soul that gets reflected through the mind in one's character. But since the mind also takes inputs from the world, it gets coloured with shades of desires and fears. So when a person values his body too much, he becomes prone to straying from the path of good.

However, another enemy of good is good itself, which can come up as an ethical dilemma. For example, there may arise a situation when one has to choose between honesty and duty towards one's kids, or when one has to choose between telling lies and saving someone's life or honour. Usually one tries to strike a balance, but there are situations when one has to give up one good for another. The choice made can hound one's conscience and leave gaping holes of guilt in one's psyche. Worse, later generations may tick off these choices without caring to understand the ideological forces working behind them.

When still in his teens, Rama was taken by the sage Viswamitra to protect his yajna from the evil forces. It was there for the first time that the young prince faced his first dilemma of whether or not to kill a female who was devilish. Initially he hesitated, but when she became more violent, he had to kill her. Much later, in a similar situation, Rama had the ears and nose of Shurpanakha cut off instead of killing her. One can thus see how there can never be a universal principle to handle dilemmas.

As mentioned earlier, holding on to dharma is often difficult because of the ethical dilemmas produced by conflicting values that are equally valid. Indeed there come situations in life when one has to face conflict between two opposing but valid course of action. Itihasa–Purana literature specialise in this kind of situation. For example, Rama had to choose between the words of his father and his mother; he had to be true as a husband and also as the king when the situation demanded that he banish Sita; he had to honour his words of protection to Sugriva, and killing an apparently innocent Bali. In all these situations Rama chose to do what his conscience, produced by his pure and unselfish mind, dictated. The greatness of *Ramayana* and *Mahabharata* really lie in handling this kind of conflicts.

The principle behind making a choice during an ethical dilemma in these scriptures is that whatever choice one may make, he will be criticised for leaving out the other. So it is meaningless to lament over the choice made. One has to have a clear goal of life and move ahead. When there is a choice between right and wrong, choose the right; and when a choice has to be made between two rights, just take up one and move forward. Cogitating and sorrowing over the left out can only make one waste his vital resources.

One may find it strange, but it is a fact that Rama–Ravana war is not really about the battle between good and evil, but it is a conflict between two different interpretations of rightness. According to Ravana, the forest belonged to his empire, and hence he could pick up any lady on whom he took a fancy. In the process he and his clan were exterminated, but he never had any remorse. On the other hand, Rama believed that as a Kshatriya prince it was his dharma to destroy the evil that casts its eye on his wife. The later poets, however, portrayed the characters of Rama and Ravana in deeper shades of white and black to impress upon the innocent minds the need to be virtuous.

The Vedic knowledge was mostly in the hands of the Brahmins, and the later Hinduism came to accept the supremacy of the Brahmins. But that is not the picture that one gets from Valmiki. For him goodness and values refined a personality universally, and hence these had nothing to do with a particular caste or gender. One thus finds Guhaka and Shabari who belonged to lower castes attaining excellence through their virtuous life. Mahavir Hanuman, whose spiritual eminence has caught the imagination of India for thousands of years, was definitely not a Brahmin, but was a bachelor, virtuous, and well versed in Vedic learning. When Sri Rama and his brother Lakshmana were moving in the forest in search of kidnapped Sita, they were spotted by the exiled king Sugiva. Afraid, he sent Mahavir Hanuman to find out the identity of the duo. Hanuman approached them and asked politely about their identity. The words and the intonations used by him charmed Sri Rama, who then softly spoke to Lakshmana praising Hanuman's art of speech,

> One who has not studied Rig, Yajur and Sama Vedas cannot speak that way. (i.e. unless a person is well educated, he cannot use good language). Surely he has studied grammar well. There is not even a little mistake in his pronunciation of words in all that he spoke.

Like Mahavir Hanuman, nearly every important character of *Ramayana* is a non-Brahmin. Eminent historians may hear whispers of class struggle in this, but it is not so. *Ramayana* only represents goodness that transcends the limits of Brahminhood, or any other caste. The core of Hinduism lies in this very fact. One has to acquire goodness by all means and be free from the limits of the body and mind.

Relevance in Present Times

A personality is shaped by the ideas and activities picked up unconsciously as a child, and acquired consciously as an adult. The ideal of India is to be good and make others good through spirituality. This could be best done by hammering the ideals in the minds of the masses from its childhood to the death bed through stories, enactment and perceptible ideals.

Sita, Rama, Lakshmana, Bharata, Mahavir Hanuman, and others, as also Ravana, Vibhishana, Meghnada, Kumbhakarna, and others are used in daily language in India to brand a character type, while relationships are measured against the backdrop of the behaviour of the characters of the *Ramayana*. Of all these characters, Sita, and Rama have come to be perceived as the individual and also the paired ideals for India. These two personalities represent the ideal and the guiding principle of every religious Hindu. Their tryst with goodness and tribulations through their suffering act as lighthouses for those willing to sail the path of righteousness without getting lost in the choppy waters of worldliness—whose other name is unrighteousness. Indeed, it is not easy to take the path of good in life, but nor it is impossible. This is one theme that one finds getting repeated in *Ramayana*. Goodness leads to blessedness, and hence one has to take it even if one has to suffer for it.

The recurring theme of the *Ramayana* is '*Ramo dwih na abhibhasate*'—Rama does not indulge in double speak (falsehood)'. That of course does not make him arrogant, as one usually finds in the society where people boast of their honesty and truthfulness to tick off others. Even when he had to give up Sita for the welfare of his kingdom he did not flinch, but when he was asked to marry a second time he refused. However, more than any other ideal role in which Sri Rama is seen, the best is his being the ideal enemy. After the killing of Ravana, he instructed all to cremate him with all honours, saying that 'enmity is there only till one is alive'. A majestic outlook towards life indeed!

The boon of Brahma to Valmiki that *Ramayana* would be an eternal creation, has come to be proved true. Hinduism will ever resonate with *Ramayana*.

MAHABHARATA

During the time of Vyasa the Hindu society (call it by any name) was in a state of ferment. Various customs, manners, castes, and religious faiths were floating around loose, while invaders and tribes were living by their fetishes and closed customs. Vyasa took all that was good in them to make those practices an integral part of Hinduism. This helped people identify themselves with the social and the religious structure of Hinduism to move up the spiritual ladder. Vyasa thus brought religion at the doorsteps of every Hindu house in the garb of stories that soon became as popular as the story of *Ramayana*.

Mahabharata is the scripture of the Hindu masses. The ideals of the Vedas and the Upanishads, and the prerequisites to aspire for them seem too remote for a common man. Until Swami Vivekananda came on the Indian spiritual stage, people did not even know that the principles of the Upanishads could be applied to daily life too. *Ramayana*, on the other hand, has characters who are too exalted, and hence their acts appear too divine to be emulated. For example, Sri Rama had to suffer one setback after another for no fault of his, but he took them in stride. The sheer power associated with such characters make one reverence them more than use them as moulds to transform one's personality. As a result, most people end up reciting the *Ramayana* the way Brahmins recited the sacred Vedas.

Mahabharata scores over these scriptures by way of having stories and characters that appear real and close to life. No character in this book is picture perfect; everyone has personality flaws, and in spite of those shortcomings the noble ones succeed in rising above the mundane to become divine. This makes one feel that spiritual values do not belong somewhere high up in the skies, but are attainable here and now.

At times these characters even make one feel superior to them, thus creating a hope for a better life. For example, Yuddhisthira, the eldest of the five Pandava brothers, was so addicted to gambling that he put his brothers and their common wife, Draupadi, at stake. It is difficult to find such gamblers even in the most profane societies. And yet, Yuddhisthira gained a bodily entry into the heaven by virtue of his other ideals. In contrast, there is the character of Shakuni who was the maternal uncle of the Kaurava princes. Shakuni was king, a master strategist, a valiant warrior and a great gambler whose stratagem led to the defeat of Yuddhisthira in the gamble match that forced the Pandavas into the exile. Shakuni, however, never struggled to get over his worldliness the way Yuddhisthira did, and so he ended up being branded a despicable character, even though he died the death of a glorious warrior in the great war.

Every sacred work has to explain and harmonise the macro and the micro of life, the universe and the man, the sacred and

111

the secular. *Mahabharata* does it with great success through many of its sections which have developed an identity for themselves. The most important of those sections is Srimad Bhagavad Gita, or simply Gita, which for its importance will be discussed in a separate section. Gita became so famous that many more sections of *Mahabharata* came to be known as various Gita. These works gave a cohesive shape to Hindu religious outlook, and in many cases, came up with newer ideals, without compromising with the Vedic truths.

Like every other sage of India, nothing much is known about Vyasa. It is believed that he was born to a great sage Parashara, who took a fancy for a boat-girl. With time he himself came to be respected as a great sage and also as a commanding scholar of the Vedas. This helped him collect the existing hymns of the Vedas and organise then into four, as mentioned in the earlier section. Later, he composed the great sacred epic, *Mahabharata* in which he poured spiritual, religious, philosophical, social and cultural wisdom of the then Hindu race around the story of a clan. Encyclopaedic in character, this is the largest religious book in the world. The sheer immensity of its sweep is best described by a popular verse, 'Whatever is there in this world to be known concerning the ways and goal of life, is there in this book; and whatever is not here is nowhere to be found.'

It is interesting to know that the practices and philosophy that Vyasa approved of in his works continues to be in vogue even today, and all that he left out, withered away slowly from the mainstream Hinduism.

The story goes that when Vyasa planned to compose *Mahabharata*, he could find no competent person to take down his dictation. So, he approached Lord Ganesha to take up this difficult task. The Lord agreed upon the condition that his pen must not stop for Vyasa to think things over. Vyasa agreed but added that the Lord must not write down any shloka (verse) without first understanding its meaning. Making use of this clause, Vyasa composed more than 8,000 profound shlokas that made even the Lord think over them to understand them correctly. This helped Vyasa gain time to compose great many shlokas for his monumental work which when complete had 1,00,000 verses.

This story hints at the depth of philosophy, religion, and spirituality that one would. *Mahabharata* begins with the story of Bharata, son of Shakuntala, who was the daughter of Viswamitra and Menaka, an *apsara*, who had been sent by the gods to tempt the sage move away from the spiritual practices. From there the story goes back in tradition, beginning with creation, and then softly narrows down to the Kuru–Pandava clan that forms the core story of this work. Being the story of the Bharata dynasty, the work came to be known as 'Bharata' (pronounced Bhaarat), or more popularly as *Mahabharata*.

Content

The Pandavas and Kauravas were cousins, who both claimed the right over the throne of Hastinapur, which had fallen vacant due to the death of King Pandu. Pandu had been struck with a curse that had made him go to the forest with his two wives. To run the kingdom, he had made his blind brother, Dhritarashtra, its regent. Pandu died in the forest when his sons, five of them, were quite young. These valiant but saintly princes came to be known as Pandavas.

After the death of their father, Pandava princes went back to Hastinapur where they had to contend with their 100 Kaurava cousins (children of Dhritarashtra), who by then had got used to the luxuries of the privileged. This led to a power struggle between the cousins in which Kauravas tried to destroy the Pandavas, who fled from the kingdom for their safety. Over the years, there were intrigues and reconciliation, gains and losses, and finally the issue came to such a head that a war had to be fought to resolve the deadlock. In that great war, armies of nearly every state of India took part. The Kaurava army outnumbered the Pandava army by eleven to seven, but the Pandava army won due to the skilful guidance of Sri Krishna, and the exceptional valour of Arjuna, who was the chief warrior of the Pandava clan.

Despite being the victors and becoming the rulers, the Pandavas had the remorse of the huge killing that had taken place for the empire. So, a time came when they left everything behind and went to the Himalayas on foot, walking through the snow of the sacred mountain till they fell dead one by one.

The intrigues, antecedents, incidents, adventures, narration, teachings, and discussions on religion and values that surround the story make the epic a phenomenal scripture. In between, there are hundreds of stories through which different ideas are explained.

It needs to be mentioned here that the discussions and stories in *Mahabharata* are in such a huge number that it is difficult to even list them, what to say then of narrating them in brief. This paper is not an overview of the great epic; it merely discusses certain core contents that shaped Hinduism. To understand the multi-dimensional aspect of Hinduism, it is essential to read this work in full.

Idea of an Imperfect World

The idea emerging from *Mahabharata* is that human beings are not expected to be perfect, nor it is expected of them to overcome their imperfections—one has to live with what one has. That, however, should not deter a person from focussing on one's core strength. Achievement in life comes through the fulfilment of strength, and never by one's futile struggle to overcome one's weaknesses. In fact, the term weakness itself is vague and misleading. When a person is judged by the standards of others, then only comes the idea of weakness. But every individual is inherently unique, and hence one cannot be, and must not be compared by how others were, or by what others did. Everyone is the measure of himself, and so it is naive to be judgemental, or to aspire to be what one is not. The strength of a chain is judged by its weakest link, but a tree is judged by the best fruits that it produces. Achievers are not like chains, but are like fruit bearing trees. They are not judged by the inconsequential acts or trivial creations of their life, but they are adored for the master acts they perform and the master pieces they produce. *Mahabharata* follows this principle with its hundreds of characters, and thus becomes the scripture of hope, inspiration, and guidance for the great and also for the small.

Difficulties in the Path of Spirituality

By focussing on individual growth, in spite of all imperfections, *Mahabharata* came to be respected as the scripture for the masses that contained realistic struggle of characters to evolve spiritually. Like *Ramayana*, *Mahabharata* too represents the urges and hopes, ideals and failures, struggle and success of the Indian race in its walk on the road to spiritual evolution. But more than the story of success, as one would expect in any idealistic work, *Mahabharata* narrates the failures and struggles that one is expected to face in life, and more so in spiritual life.

For example, there is the story of the great maverick sage Viswamitra who was a *Kshatriya* king, but because of a feud with

Vasistha, a great sage of his times, he gave up his kingdom and took to spirituality with the intention of outgrowing the sage. Viswamitra performed intense *tapasya*, and by the powers acquired through it, he had Vasistha's son killed! Thereafter, he again performed *tapasya*, but was tempted by the Divine dancer Menaka, from whom he gave birth to Shakuntala. Losing all his powers thus, he started afresh, but circumstances made him create a new heaven that was of no use to any. Thus continued the rise of the sage through *tapasya*, and also his fall through anger, arrogance, and lust. Finally a time came when nothing could swerve him from attaining the heights of spiritual wisdom. This resulted in his great contribution towards the Vedic corpus, and also in gaining the Gaytri mantra through spiritual revelation, which is recited daily by most Hindus all over the world.

This story is not a standalone in *Mahabharata*. There are many such stories that give glimpses of the difficulties in the path of religion. But unlike a novel, this epic does not wallow in the sty of failure, but smiles in the freshness of outgrowing the inevitable.

Mukti for All

The spiritual ideals presented in *Mahabharata* are same as in the Vedas. The recurring theme of the work is that everything in the universe is the manifestation of divine, although the individual consciousness associated with them does not allow one to have the realisation, or even the basic understanding of this truth. Human beings, by virtue of their evolved intelligence, have the capability to realise this truth, and thus to become what they truly are—one with God. Realisation of this truth, known as mukti, is be all and do all for everyone.

The epic stresses this ideal again and again through its different stories and discussions. However, *Mahabharata* makes a major departure from the Vedic tradition at this point. Unlike the Vedic tradition that stressed on the hierarchy of spiritual competence in which the Brahmins were the highest by the virtue of their knowledge of the Vedas, *Mahabharata* stresses that anyone can attain mukti by being true to oneself, since divinity is the inherent nature of every created being.

Mahabharata thus became the first work to break through the barriers of caste, creed, and sex for the pursuit of spiritual goal, which in earlier times was reserved only for the sages. One finds women philosophers like Sulabha, courtesan like Pingala, a butcher like Dharma Vyadha, and the hawker like Tuladhara as being spiritually eminent. This shows that there can be no social precondition for spiritual enlightenment. In the story of Dharma Vyadha, there was a young sage who by the virtue of his *tapasya* attained great powers. Gloating over his powers, he was humbled by a housewife who could read his mind and treat his powers with indifference simply by being true to her husband and household responsibilities. She then sent this sage to the butcher who sold meat, but was established in the highest spiritual knowledge by virtue of his performing his caste-based duties with respect. This opened the eyes of the sage, who realised that anyone could gain enlightenment by being true to one's duties. The importance did not lie in 'becoming', but in 'being'.

Dharma—a Way of Life

Those who were leading a life in the world, away from the all-renouncing life of sages and monks, too could evolve spiritually. To do so, or to attain *purusartha* (*dharma, artha, kama, moksha*), *Mahabharata* suggests practice of dharma—the way of life. For a gross mind, life is about being parasitical, but for an elevated mind, the way of life is dictated by the principles of giving space to others. The set of practices that makes one give space to others is known as values. When these values are corollaries to spiritual truths, these are known as dharma, otherwise these are just mores. *Mahabharata* discusses dharma in its entirety, and its recurring theme is *yato dharmah tato jayah*—success comes to the idealist.

This may sound naive since people with noble traits are invariably seen to suffer in life. But no scripture ever looks at life in short terms. To them, life is a continuity that extends beyond death, and hence quick fixes, easy grabbing, etc. are treated as shortcuts to destruction. However, *Mahabharata* neither describes destruction of the clever, nor the success of the idealist; it merely describes the struggle of different characters to hold on to dharma in spite of weaknesses and occasional falls born out of compelling situation in life, and at times, even out of sheer demand of passions. The general refrain is that to give in to the demands of the body is wrong, but to hold on to dharma is the way to spiritual evolution.

The sages believe that anyone who follows dharma can never face a mental crisis. For example, in spite of facing adversities all their lives, the Panadavas, and many other great characters never suffered mental crisis. They even accepted death and personal loss with grace. Today's crisis in the society is the crisis of dharma. People are not willing to do what they are supposed to do, which ultimately makes them mental wrecks.

Like a master diamantaire, Vyasa took up the crude diamond of existence, and then cut and polished it to reveal the hidden beauty that sparkles through the innumerable facets of dharma. The entire work is essentially a work on dharma that leaves no aspect of it untouched.

Many definitions of dharma have been given in the book, of which one is, '*Prajna* (Right intellect) makes one adhere to scriptural instructions, which in turn makes one practice dharma. *Hri* (lit. modesty, sense of shame, decorum, decency) is the most important virtue of dharma. A modest person stays away from sinful activities. This increases his wealth, status, and recognition in the society. The more one has these, the more he is a man. A shameless or a stupid person is neither a man nor a woman. He is not fit to practice dharma. He is fallen and wretched.' *Udyoga Parva* (72.35–37).

However, there is no simplistic codification of dharma here, as one would expect from a scripture. Nor are the acts of commission and omission categorised in black and white. At one place it says that one must not follow a dharma simply because many are following it; one must think of the consequences of an action, good or bad, and only then he should take up that path. That is the right dharma. For example, the decision of the five Pandavas to marry Draupadi raised serious ethical question. To that Yudhistira replied that in matters of dharma, precedence was important, which in this case, was there; there had been polyandrous sages in the past. He further added that he could not transgress the instructions of his mother, and also that he was established in truth and so his tongue could never speak improper or untrue words. This episode explains the complexities involved in defining dharma, since it demands precedence, purity, and values. However, a person with impure motive does not have the moral authority to pass off his desires as dharma.

Mahabharata is a realistic scripture that does not try to hide the cruel face of life behind the facade of ideals. When Draupadi was dragged to the royal court after Yudhisthira had lost her in the gamble, she cried piteously and asked everyone present there whether or not adharma was being committed through that act.

119

The responses were quite interesting: Duryodhana was convinced that dharma was on his side; his own brother Vikarna believed that it was wrong; and Bhisma added pathetically to Draupadi, 'In a crisis situation, dharma is overpowered by the powerful!' So, to expect others to be virtuous is naivety.

At times *Mahabharata* reads like an epic by a master poet who lets the line of good and bad thin out. There are descriptions when even the best of characters let go of their ideals to achieve their goal. Jarasandha and Duryodhana were killed unethically by the Panadvas at the suggestion of Sri Krishna. A large many moral transgressions were committed by both parties during the *Mahabharata* war that included killing of the great and respected too. Even Bhishma, the grandsire of the clan, was laid out in the battle field by Arjuna through a trick.

Looking closely at all this, it appears as if *Mahabharata* treats life as importantly as any spiritual ideal. It repeatedly talks of non-violence as the highest virtue, *ahimsa paramo dharmah*, even higher than truth. The practice of truth leads to inclusiveness, but non-violence is inclusiveness. So to treat one's life as precious, particularly to lead a religious life, is fair enough. Continuing this idea, *Mahabharata* details conditions when one can tell lies—during fun, to one's beloved during intimacy, while arranging marriage, to save one's life, to save someone else's life, to save one's loss of everything, and to save someone else's complete loss. There is also discussion on how one can give up an ideal temporarily to save one's life. This is known as *apad dharma*, the dharma of emergency.

In one of the popular stories, the great sage Viswamitra stole dead dog's meat from the house of an outcaste to sate his hunger. When challenged, the sage replied that if he died of hunger, nothing good was to come out of it, but if he survived by taking forbidden food, he could perform *prayascitta* (penance) and be pure again. This of course does not give a person the license to go wild. Under normal conditions, one is supposed to stick to one's dharma strictly.

The dharma of an individual depends on his varna (caste), the ashrama (station of life), and the particular employment that one has. In addition, everyone is supposed to follow a common code of conduct as a human being. All these constitute *achara*, the code of conduct of life. Dharma is the genus of which the *varnashrama dharma* is the species. Without the concept of dharma, the relevance of caste and order of life is meaningless. The very uniqueness of the Hindu society lies in its holding on to *varnashrama dharma*, which was first raised in this epic. This will be elaborated in the section on the law books.

Destiny—the Sum Total of Karma

Like many other philosophical principles, the law of karma was hinted at in the Upanishads, but was elaborated in the *Mahabharata*. This theory later became a prominent model to explain everything in the universe.

Law of karma is based on the cause-effect relationship, but unlike the general understanding that every effect must have a cause, the law of karma builds on the premise that every cause will have an effect, and it is inviolable. Everything that one does by way of action, thoughts, or words form karma (lit. action), that act as seed to bear crops at appropriate time. When taken to the extreme, it was said that 'as a calf finds out its mother cow, in the same way the effect finds its doer.'

This may not be literally true, but the idea that every karma leaves a *samskara* (lit. impression) on the mind that makes one repeat them in future with due consequences, is universally accepted in

Hinduism. To overcome one's unwanted samskara, one has to do *tapasya* (austerities), and *prayaschitta* (penances), without which one sinks lower till he ends up being a brute.

One may not agree to this model, but one can never fail to appreciate its profundity. Law of karma puts the onus of good or bad in life on the individual, and not on God, nor on some blind chance. The strength required to accept that we alone are responsible for all the bad or good that happen to us, is mind boggling. Hinduism is not a religion of gods and goddesses, but is the religion of the individual. One's fall, rise, and liberation is one's own doing.

Law of karma does not prescribe passivity or pessimism. It rather exhorts one to carve one's destiny through intense karma. Going by the principle that the solution of a problem lies in the system itself, law of karma emphasises the role of an individual in all the negativity that might be surrounding him.

Destiny is the sum total of karma done in the past. The outcome of an action is a consequence of both present karma, and the past (destiny). But *Mahabharata* does not take sides on the issue of self-effort and destiny. At places it is said that the destiny makes people work in such a way that the destiny gets fulfilled, and at other times it is said that the destiny bows before a firm resolve to act in a particular way. There is the story of princess Savitri who was married to Satyavan who had lost his kingdom and was living in a forest with his blind parents. Satyavan was destined to die within a short period. Savitri had come to know about it through a sage, but she kept it a secret. On the fateful day she went to the forest with Satyavan. When Yama (God of death) came to take away the soul of the fated, Savitri kept walking behind him since it was her dharma as a wife to follow her husband. Yama tried to dissuade her in many ways that included giving her various boons, but she continued following her dead husband on one pretext or the other. Finally her persistent effort, prayer and presence of mind, made Yama go soft, and he allowed Satyavan to get back his life. One thus realises that the possibility of karma getting changed is always there.

On the other hand, there is the story of Draupadi's brother who was born of a yajna to kill Drona, the warrior-teacher of the clan. When the prince came to learn the art of warfare from him, Drona agreed to teach him even though he knew that this may lead him to death in the hands of the prince. But Drona felt that if he was destined to die in the hands of the prince, there could be no way to defy the inevitable. So then why give up his dharma as a teacher and gain infamy!

There is also the story of some sages who were born as birds. When still birdling, they were caught in a great forest fire, to which they agreed that death must be warded off till it could be. They had the option of entering a rat hole, but they argued themselves out of it saying, 'ignoble death was to be shunned'. So they all prayed to Agni, the fire God, who let them off.

These stories may appear to have conflicting messages, but these are in fact not so. These all focus on the importance of holding on to dharma. If death comes while performing one's duties, one would at least have the satisfaction of having lived the right kind of life. *Mahabharata* thus does not approve of disgraceful life, dishonourable death, and not even ignominious acts.

Other conflicting issues like free will and God's will, truth and non-violence, etc. are dealt in the same way. The epic does not take sides. Instead, it narrates stories to highlight both aspects and then narrows down to show the importance of staying true to one's way of life, whatever that might be.

New Gods and Avatars

The great contribution of *Mahabharata* to Hindu religion lies in its presenting new Gods like Brahma, Vishnu, Shiva, and Krishna. In the earlier sections it was mentioned how God is perceived both as formless, and also with form. Since God is not an entity, the idea of God with form and qualities, is like giving a mask to the infinite. It is like offering chocolate in different shapes; any shape is as good as any other as far as chocolate is concerned. Kids may quarrel over the different shapes, but the grownups would know that the same chocolate was being offered in those shapes. Similar is the case when God is seen as with form and qualities—it is the same God who is worshipped through different names and forms.

It was mentioned in the section on the Vedas how gods like Indra, Varuna and others were taken up as the mask of the infinite, and how hymns offered to them describe the traits of God, the infinite. But because of various worldly traits that these gods came to represent, they could never get the adoration due to God. So Vyasa broke the existing moulds to come up with new masks on the infinite. Of these, Vishnu, who was not much famous in the Vedic times, and nor did he have negative traits, became the favourite. Building on certain traits of Vishnu, like taking up various forms, Vyasa poured the idea of infinite through his personality. In the process he also transformed the idea of Vishnu taking up many forms with the idea of incarnation, avatara. This was a great concept contributed and developed by Vyasa in *Mahabharata* that was detailed with great care in the Puranas.

The idea of Vishnu incarnating in different forms that included a boar, fish, lion-man, sages, Sri Rama, Sri Krishna and others implied that a spiritual aspirant could take up any of these forms, or even any other exalted personality and worship him as God. This is perfectly fine, since God is neither a personality, nor an entity, and hence one can always see the chosen personality as a repository of qualities of God. Thus one could see Buddha as an incarnation of Vishnu, with the qualities of love, compassion, and knowledge fully manifest in him. In turn, this helped more and more people become spiritual since they could now choose from amongst millions of the incarnations/forms of God that suited their taste and mentality.

As with Vishnu, the idea of Shiva as the infinite God was also added following the same principle of spirituality. With time, Vishnu and Shiva became the two prominent God of the Hindus. Unlike the Vedic period when only sages could compose hymns, now even ordinary people from any caste, creed, or sex could compose songs and hymns in the name of God. Thus the floodgates of spirituality were opened by Vyasa for all.

Mahabharata also introduced the concept of Shakti worship. There were a few hymns in the Vedas dedicated to female principles of God, and there was also the practices of Tantra outside the Vedic code. Vyasa took them up in one sweep and came up with the worship of Durga and other female divinities in the same way as Vishnu and Shiva were worshipped. The Puranas then consolidated these divinities to define the worship pattern of the Hindus.

Relevance in Presents Times

Mahabharata collected and consolidated the religious and spiritual ideals that had grown in India till then, and gave them a fresh spread by filtering out the vestigial. Anyone patient enough to read the entire *Mahabharata* would be struck by the simplicity of its language, its wide outreach to life, and the depth of its ideas. This sacred epic heralded a new era in the Indian spiritual tradition that was later taken forward by the Puranas to come up with the evolved Hinduism that we see today.

The innumerable characters of the story have entered the daily vocabulary of the Indians to compare persons with them, and to make suggestions to make improvements in one's quality of life. At the same time, a large many characters and stories are looked up to during crisis situation. *Mahabharata* is thus a living scripture that makes real time and real life contribution. It is not the scripture for the dead, but for the alive.

Its grand message, of course, is not to look at one's weaknesses, which will always be there, and one can never overcome them fully. So one needs to focus on the path that one has taken up and keep walking, in spite of the stumbles, till he becomes one with God in this very life.

THE PURANAS

The Puranas were composed to suit the needs of the masses for an easy understanding of the spiritual truths. Despite their mythological nature, they discuss philosophy, ethics, and rituals of the Hindus in detail. These are eighteen in number and form the mythological base of the Hindus. These have around 5.5 lakh verses through which the popular stories of gods and goddesses are described. The most popular of these books is *Srimad Bhagavata Purana* which deals mainly with the story of Sri Krishna. *Shiva Maha Purana* is another popular work centring Lord Shiva.

The synthetic approach of the Hindus meant that they did not consider anything secular, i.e. away from God—all that was, was manifestation of the Divine. Play of religion was seen everywhere, and everything was looked at religiously. Every branch of knowledge like art, science, music, performing arts, sculpture—everything was perceived as a means to the worship of the Divine.

Even the apparently erotic motifs that one sees in some temples, or the love songs of Radha-Krishna that are popularly heard all over the country, are offerings of creative minds to God in the forms that they could best offer. It is impossible for the untrained minds and crude eyes to understand the expression of the Divine through these, the way one cannot understand the finer points of art.

When the Divine is expressed through literature, it is known as Purana.

The Vedas and the Upanishads contain core spiritual truths that were realised by the sages, while *Ramayana* and *Mahabharata* present religion through literature in which the protagonists are human beings through whom the play of the Divine is expressed. In Puranas, the spiritual truths are maintained as in the Vedas, and stories are maintained as in *Ramayana–Mahabharata*, but the protagonist is God and his many forms, while human characters play secondary roles. The literal meaning of the word Purana is 'traditional stories', but the derived meaning is 'traditional religious stories that remain ever fresh'. *Ramayana* and *Mahabharata* too are at times referred to as Purana, but because of the predominance of human character, these are more popularly known as Itihasa. Seen historically, some Puranic stories are to be found in the Vedas itself that were known as *narasamsi*. These stories were later taken up by sages and were developed into full-size Puranas with the help of their own liberal contributions.

It was mentioned in the previous section on *Mahabharata* how performance of dharma was presented as the key to religious life. But a race committed to religion needs a more direct, deeper and committed approach towards spirituality. *Mahabharata* is good as a timeless scripture, but the devoted Hindu race needed a more intense guide for the spiritual journey that would be comprehensible to the ordinary minds. This need was fulfilled by the Puranas. The relationship between the Puranas and *Mahabharata* is same as that between the Upanishads and the Vedas. The Vedas show the way to gaining eminence in this life and the next through yajna, while the Upanishads talk about gaining spiritual enlightenment as the only goal of life. In the same way, *Mahabharata* shows the way to eminence in both the worlds through the practise of dharma, but the Puranas talk about gaining devotion to the Lord as the goal of life. The slight difference between the Upanishads and the Puranas is that the Upanishads talk of core Vedanta (also known as the path of knowledge), while the Puranas talk primarily of bhakti (devotion) through stories. However, all these scriptures have common elements in them. Their difference lies in their emphasising some aspects more than other.

In *Srimad Bhagavatam*, which is a Purana, there is this story about Vyasa who once sat pensive even though he had already collected the Vedas and had organised them into four, and had composed *Mahabharata* in 1,00,000 verses, as mentioned in the earlier sections. At that time, the divine sage Narada chanced to come to him, and on hearing about Vyasa's inner turmoil said that since he had not written about the glories of God, and how to have devotion towards him, he was not yet at peace. 'You have not broadcast the sublime and spotless glories of God. The philosophy that does not talk about the Lord is considered worthless, and are considered by the saints to be like the lowly pilgrimage for crows (not fit for swans).' (*Bhagavatam* 1.5.8). Vyasa then got down to composing the Puranas that were dedicated to describing the nature, form, and glories of God as means to spiritual evolution.

The tradition says that Vyasa composed eighteen Puranas in 5,00,000 verses, but scholars are definite that most of these were standardised later. This is quite possible since these stories used to be narrated at various kinds of gatherings, and these were not maintained as strictly as the words of the Vedas were maintained. So the possibility of editing, additions and standardisation, keeping the core intact, is very much there. However, this does not affect the uniformity of character and outlook of the Puranas.

The goal of the narratives in the Puranas is to lead a person towards highest spiritual enlightenment through mythological stories, philosophy, ethics, and rituals—in that order of importance. According to a popular saying Puranas deal with five topic—creation, dissolution, genealogies, stories about Manu (the first born in every new cycle of creation), and stories of some dynasties.

In addition, these also discuss traditions, philosophy, religious, and social issues, duties of different castes, sacraments, customs in general, eatables and non-eatables, duties of women, rites and rituals, ceremonies, penances, pilgrimage, descriptions of hells, karma, images and idols, etc. Thus each of the 18 Puranas covers every aspect of a Hindu's individual, social and religious life, and hence followers of any of these Puranas do not have to study Upanishads (for philosophy), Smritis (for good conduct), or Tantras (for rituals). That is how the Puranas became the unquestioned rulers of a Hindu's life for the last 2,000 years or so.

The stretch of the Puranas on the divinities resulted in absorbing stories of various Gods and Goddess, which in turn had tremendous impact on the followers of different sects, who all had at least one Purana marked as their sacred book. Of the 18 Puranas, *Srimad Bhagavatam*, centring the divine life of Sri Krishna, is the most famous Purana in which the birth and deeds of Sri Krishna are recounted. These stories impacted Indian psyche strongly, and later sage-poets developed different aspects of Sri Krishna's divine life into independent literature.

Other Puranas narrate stories about Vishnu, Shiva, and Shakti in which stories from *Ramayana* and *Mahabharata* are used freely, but composed differently. Two popular religious work of the Hindus, *Adhyatma Ramayana* and *Sri Sri Chandi*, are from two Puranas. These two works are recited daily in countless Hindu families devoted to Sri Rama and Shakti (Durga, Kali, etc.) respectively.

Later, 18 Upa-Puranas (subsidiaries) having around 5,00,000 verses were added to the existing literature. These could not become as popular as the main Puranas, but they did leave a strong impression on the Hindu society.

The innumerable stories of the Divine make many think the Puranas as myths, as the word is commonly understood. But this is not correct. Unlike a mythological narrative, the Puranas are religious texts like Bible, in which spiritual truths are presented in the story form. Symbolic stories like Adam's fall from the heaven that one gets in Christianity or Islam, abound the Puranas, but they never lose sight of the highest spiritual truths of the Vedas. For example, Sri Krishna is described to have been born in a prison from where his father managed to take him away when he found the prison gates open miraculously, and the guards asleep. Within a few days of this great escape, Putana, a deadly demon, was sent to kill the baby Krishna by suckling him with poisoned breast milk. Krishna, who was barely a few days old at the time, killed her effortlessly. From that time on, he went on killing a countless number of demons and negative personalities. In between killing them, he would go around doing mischief, and frolicking around the village belles.

The Puranas are scriptures, and hence all that they discuss about the world must not be taken literally. Every Purana has some historical truth at its centre, but not much attention should be paid to their historical, geographic, or scientific descriptions.

These descriptions are meant to give a feel of immensity and also subtlety involved in creation by God. The aim of these is to describe the glory of God and not the description of creation's vanities.

Great sages and prophets perceive the Divine in the depths of their inner world, in which some inputs from the external world too find an entry. This is the meeting ground of the Divine and the world in which the world plays a trivial role. Thus when one reads the prowess of Sri Rama in the battlefield, one has to remember that this prowess is not to be taken literally, since scriptures are not historical records but a contemplative work centring the Divine, built on the worldly ideas so that people can identify with them. Aspiring devotees read and contemplate on these stories to make the journey of their identity from the world to God. With time, the successful among them come up with their own realisations, teachings and narrations.

Content

The idea behind these stories is to convey the nature and essence of God through his incarnation in any of the forms (mentioned later) that he may choose to take up. God is ever established in the naturalness of his strength, power, wisdom, knowledge, etc. The best way to impress such qualities of God on the common minds is to come up with stories that would be so awe inspiring that a person would ever remember them.

The Supreme Love

On the same lines, the popular stories about Sri Krishna playing with Radha and other gopis (the village damsels) are meant to give the idea of what it means to have divine love for God. The technical term for this kind of love is *para* bhakti (the supreme love). In that state the devotee forgets himself, the world around him, and the social restrictions that hold him with the society. These stories are indeed descriptions of a very high state of spiritual longing and ecstasy as one finds with Sufi saints like Rabiah al-Adawiyah, or with the Christian mystics like Saint Teresa of Avilla.

Aspects of Inner World

The external world is experienced through the five senses, and one reacts towards these sense data through five organs of action, with the mind acting as the mediation agent in both cases. A non-spiritual person works out a pattern from the chaos entering through his senses, and then acts upon it to have a satisfactory life.

For a spiritual person, the physical world is secondary in importance to the rich inner spiritual world that is formed within him by concretisation of ideas through deep contemplation and meditation. This should not make one conclude that God and his divine sport, as described in scriptures, are products of imagination. For spiritual persons, truth about God is much more real and true than the world is to a common man. Since mind is the medium of perception for the external and also the inner world, it would be unfair to accept one as true, and the other one as false.

Those who love to see God as having qualities like compassion, want to see God as his own and also want to form some kind of relationship like father, mother, master, beloved, etc. with him, without letting go of the idea that he is God. This requires constant prayer and contemplation on the qualities of God, his divine sport, and his innumerable forms. The Puranas fulfil this need by covering aspects of devotion. People not familiar with the inner world of spirituality find such descriptions incomprehensible, irrational, and fantastical, although these are not so.

So what about hallucinations, since a hallucinating person too takes his fantasies as real? The answer is that the mentally challenged fail to accept the world the way it is. Spiritual persons, on the other hand, accept the world as it is, and they behave towards it with much more compassion than is possible for even the most noble. The character of spiritual persons become so exalted that one feels attracted towards them spontaneously, whereas people are generally wary of approaching the mentally sick.

Interestingly, for both spiritual and non-spiritual persons the idea of 'me' and 'mine' play important roles in their respective worlds. For spiritual persons, these two ideas revolve around God, while for the non-spiritual these stay identified with persons and objects of this world. Spirituality is thus a short journey in which a person moves his identity from God's creation to God himself. This journey can take less than a second, or may take many lives, depending on the intensity of one's desire to complete the journey from the created to creator.

God—His Power and Incarnations

The world around us, with all its good, bad, and ugly, is a fact that can never be denied. At times, it also makes one wonder wherefrom all this came, and where it will ultimately end up. This question is difficult to answer, since no one was present when the creation bloomed. And yet, like a virulent virus, this riddle keeps coming up, which is addressed by scientists, philosophers, and sages variously.

The Puranas accept every theory of creation that has been worked out by the Hindu philosophers. Of these, the more popular one is described with elegance, while others find a shorter mention. The recurring idea is that God created this universe through his power in which he created objects and life, and let everything work out its destiny.

Since the Vedas had not named God, but had only hinted at his possible qualities, sages of later times looked at God differently. Of these, Narayana came to be accepted more universally, which later got identified with Vishnu. The Puranas describe God (Vishnu) acting differently during creation, sustenance, and dissolution as Brahma, Vishnu, and Shiva. Thus, Vishnu, who was an ordinary God in the Vedas, working under the leadership of Indra, came to be seen as the sustainer of the universe, and also as the God.

By its nature, the world has good and not so good, in varying proportions. The good is defined as the minds that derive their strength from the knowledge of spirituality, and the not so good derive their strength through existential means. The first one is known as godly, and the second one, *asuri*. The *asuri* have the tendency to overpower all that comes its way, thus creating a conflict situation with the godly. In a travesty of justice, the good always get beaten in the hands of the not-so-good. This creates a loss of balance that demands special interference by the Divine in his various forms to stabilise the world.

It is in the nature of things to lose orderliness with time, and hence the tendency of goodness to decay in the world too is an inviolable fact. So, even after God sets things right, the world tends to get into decay mode, soon enough, that continues to grow with time, till God intervenes again. The forms taken up by God in the affairs of the world are known as avatara—incarnation.

Incarnations happen only with Vishnu. His ten popular avataras are: Matsya (The Fish), Kurma (The Tortoise), Varaha (The Boar), Narasimha (The Man-Lion), Vamana (The Dwarf), Parasurama (the axe wielder Rama), Sri Rama, Sri Krishna, Buddha, and Kalki (the warrior). This list is not fixed; at other places the

Puranas talk of 24 avataras, and also talk of infinite number of incarnations. The basic principle behind every avatara, even for those who are yet to come, is to bring stability between materialism and spirituality.

A popular verse describes the idea and power behind incarnation:

> Appearing in bodies of a fish, tortoise, human, etc., O Lord! You exhibit activities impossible for such creatures to perform. These bodies are therefore not made of material elements, but are incarnations of your supreme personality.

This verse exhibits the unlimited power in the form of strength, knowledge, compassion, or any other such virtue, associated with an incarnation.

The doctrine of incarnation of the Puranas is unique. The *vedantins* believe in an eternal God (Isvara), while the Buddhists and the Sankhyas (an important school of Hindu philosophy) believe only in a God, who was earlier a man but became God through spiritual practices. The Puranas reconcile these two positions, and say that the perfected person is nothing but the *nitya* Isvara (eternal God), who with the help of his own maya takes up that form. This also gives scope for an infinite number of avatara in Hinduism, as opposed to the Christian or Islamic concepts of limited number of messengers of God.

Unlike incarnations, there are also cases of manifestation of Brahma, Shiva, and Shakti when they appear before an individual or the collective, in response to prayers to fulfil their needs that can range from simple greed to life threatening crisis. By describing the fulfilment of such prayers, the Puranas try to increase the faith of the devout towards their chosen ideal.

Masks on the Infinite

By the time the last of the Puranas were standardised, these had grown like a massive roaring river from the rivulet of mythological stories of the Vedas. The principle was to superimpose spiritual qualities of the Divine on suitable characters. The use of such characters as masks on the infinite had begun with the Vedas, and had later grown in precision with *Ramayana–Mahabharata*. But the Puranas outdid all of them by perfecting the art of using masks on the Divine. More than that, the scope for future masks in the form of avatara, was permanently placed in the Hindu religion. It was now a step to convert anything into the Divine.

Religious Freedom and New Divinities

The ultimate of freedom in religion was started by the Puranas. The power to frame ideas in religion went from the hands of the spiritual elites to the masses, with the consequence that weird concepts made weed-like growth in Hinduism. This unleashed the dark side of freedom. As in democracy, anyone with a voice could say the most unacceptable thing, and pass it as valid. This was to be the bane of Hinduism that degraded it in the eyes of the critics and the votaries alike.

On the brighter side, the freedom accorded by the Puranas contributed mightily by creating newer formats of spiritual practices, of which the most important was a massive growth of the Bhakti movement during Islamic rule. The Puranas acted as the bridge between the Vedic principles and the practices that began in the last millennia. For example, it was mentioned in the section on the Vedas how the sages formed a relation with the Divine as friend, dancer, child, etc. This was concretised in the Puranas, and popularised by the Bhakti movement in which Krishna came to be worshipped as hapless baby, a frolicking kid, and as young lover. In all such cases, the idea was to develop a divine intimacy with God in which the devotee did not want anything material from him, since he was a baby, or a kid, or a passionate lover.

The deep emotions involved with Krishna, Vishnu, Shiva, Durga, and others meant that the principal gods of the Vedic pantheon like Indra and Varuna were permanently superseded by them. Of the Puranic gods, some were from the Vedic period, and some were later additions. In the early Vedic period, Vishnu was the God of fertility and productivity, who could take up various forms and could vanquish enemies with ease. In the Puranas, Vishnu became the all-powerful God. Similarly, Rudra was the God of death who was not allowed the rights of Vedic gods. In the Puranic period, he was given the personality that combined Pasupati (probably of Indus valley origin), and Siva (popular in South India). The popular stories about Lord Shiva centre the personalities of both.

The Puranic period is specially famous for the rise of female divinities like Lakshmi, Durga, Kali, and Parvati. Although hymns like *Devi Suktam* are there in the Vedas that pray to female divinity, and there is also the mention of Uma Haimvati (later identified with Durga) in the *Kena Upanisad*, but it was through the Puranas that these personalities got their extolled position and popularity. Shaiva mythology places goddess Parvati, the consort of Shiva, as one half of his body, while Vaishnavites place the Goddess Lakshmi in the heart of Vishnu. All this are meant to depict the non-separateness of God and his power.

With time, Rama and Krishna became as famous as Brahma, Vishnu, Shiva and Shakti. Later, Brahma lost importance, and thus the remaining five became the ruling gods of Hindu religion. This resulted in the rise of Vaishnavism (worship of Vishnu,

Rama, and Krishna), Shaivism, and Shakta traditions, along with their offshoots, that cover the entire Hindu culture today. The devotional songs that abound the country, literature, art, sculptor, etc. represent these three traditions in various forms. Shiva as Nataraj, Sri Krishna as playful God, Kali as destroyer of evil and innumerable such motifs are derived directly from the Puranas. So much so, people took liberties with these images, and had localised names (sometimes even comic) added to their favourite deities. Thus Shiva is worshipped at various places with a name like Baidyanath, Mahakal, Pasupatinath, etc. prefixed to him, and some red light areas have even Chhinal Hanuman (the wrongdoer Hanuman) for themselves.

The Role of Bhakti

The simple doctrine of bhakti, illustrated and stated through the lives of saints and kings in the Puranas replaced the complicated Vedic rituals. Bhakti has been discussed in such detail in the Puranas that to understand bhakti one has to study these sacred books. The Puranas were meant for the ordinary people who could not understand high philosophy and who could not study the Vedas. Indeed, only very few can understand and appreciate, far less live and move, in the grandeur of Vedanta, the true philosophy of the Hindus. So, study of the Puranas, listening to sacred recitals of scriptures, and narrating the transcendent *lila*s (divine play) of the Lord became an important part of sadhana for the devotees.

The Puranas have a tendency to extol one particular God, while apparently making others seem inferior. For example, in *Siva Purana*, Lord Shiva is highly praised, while an inferior position is given to Lord Vishnu. On the other hand, in *Vishnu Purana*, Lord Vishnu is highly praised, while an inferior position is given to Lord Shiva. Although this has resulted in a lot of heartburn among sects, these are in fact meant to increase the faith of the devotees in their particular Ishta Devata (chosen deity); and the principle that these Gods are in essence one and the same keeps running through the Puranas.

Image Worship

The concept of image worship first finds mention in the Puranas. The sacrificial altars of the Vedic times were replaced by the idols, and the *chaitya*s (places of religious assembly) gave way to the temples. This automatically resulted in a huge web of rituals that trapped within itself the entire Vedic ideas of yajna, prayers, gift making, etc. The unending and incomprehensible rituals that one sees everywhere in Hinduism today are result of this development.

Idea of Hell

A greater emphasis was put on ethical teachings than on metaphysical speculations. Ideas regarding law of karma, rebirth, heaven and hell became crystallised forever in the Puranas. In fact, the credit of inventing all sorts of hells (which is an alien concept in the early scriptures of India) goes to the Puranas. In most of these hells, men are continually tortured, but they never die, and thus suffer for a long period till their bad karmas get worked out, after which they are reborn in a fresh body.

Svadharma

One great contribution of the Puranas was the introduction of humanising virtues and actions conducive to the welfare of the entire creation as a mode of spiritual practice. Thus *saucha* (cleanliness), *seva* (service to others), *ahimsa* (non-violence) and such other universal virtues, were codified as *svadharma* in the Puranas, and people started practicing these virtues as sadhana (spiritual practice). The practice of truth and non-violence by Gandhiji, and service to the mankind by Swami Vivekananda are good examples of *sadharana* dharma becoming *svadharma*.

Of these virtues, purity as a paramount spiritual practice came to be the bane of Hindu society. People who cannot go deeper into ideas took purity to mean physical purity (including relationships). This led to obsessive disorders that resulted in untouchability, child marriage, helplessness of widows, neglect of masses, etc.

Relevance in Present Times

People take to religion either as a way of life, or to acquire some material gains in life. Those who want to take up spiritual enlightenment as the goal of life, for them sacred texts like Upanishads are the guide. But those who have shades of materialism within them, and those who treat life as more important than going beyond life, they have to depend on popular religious texts like Puranas, since these accept human frailties as they are, and then softly lead them to higher reaches of religion through stories, ideals, and promises of a better life.

One may find many of the Puranic stories outlandish, but one has to remember that Hinduism survived the onslaughts of the cruel entirely because of them. The religious ideals were highly diluted in them, and at times these were not even recognisable, but it was due to this thinning of the ideals that these could float freely in every strata of the Hindu society and then help it face the crisis of its inner psyche, as also give strength to struggle for survival against alien culture. It was a commendable job performed by the Puranas for more than a 1,000 years now.

Relevance of a particular Puranic story may diminish with changed times, but the core truths around which the stories are composed, will always remain relevant. This also means that the external form may change, but these can never go away permanently till even a single man has human emotions, weaknesses, and temptations. Since creation means imperfection, the Puranas are here to stay till there is creation to take care for the spiritually weak.

Of course, new Puranas will have to be written to suit the contemporary minds.

The Precious Scripture

GITA

Hinduism is not a simplistic religion that can be defined and described in a few words. The vastness and majesty of its scriptures can be best compared to an unchartable and unfathomable ocean that cannot be mapped entirely, but whose essence can be known by tasting a sip of it. As can be seen from the preceding sections, it is difficult even for the learned to master the entire range of Vedas –Upanishads–Puranas–Itihasa. What to say then of a common Hindu who neither has time, nor inclination to even go through them! So there was a need for a short work that would contain the import of all the scriptures, even if that be in mere seed form.

Srimad Bhagavad Gita (popularly known as Gita) took that exalted position.

According to a popular verse, the Upanishads are the essence of the Vedas, and Gita is the essence of the Upanishads. Thus Gita is the ultimate handbook of Hindu religion, spirituality, philosophy, ethics, myths (in embryo state), worldview, etc. Practically nothing has been added in Hindu religion after Gita, and sans Mother worship and Tantra (which is a fringe scripture), there is nothing of Hindu religion that has not been touched upon, synthesised, and aligned in this small book of 700 verses in 18 chapters. It is amazing how such a small book could bring out the majesty of such a vast religion without leaving out anything.

This kind of composition requires a timeless genius, which Vyasa was. Whether consciously or coincidentally, Vyasa put all his talents and poetic skills to come up with this wonder of a scripture that is like a priceless necklace in which spiritual outlooks are woven like gems in the thread of the spiritual truth that 'God alone is True'.

It was mentioned in the section on *Mahabharata* how Kaurava and Pandavas, who were cousins-turned-enemies, went to battle out their claim over the kingdom. In that war, all the great warriors of the country had joined one of the two sides depending on their preference and priority. This had created a situation in which relatives, friends, associates and the respected elders were pitted against each other in that holy war, popularly known as *Mahabharata* war. The war was called holy because the battle lines were drawn on the principle of rightness, and not by greed or hatred that are the two impelling forces in the world.

The chief warrior of the Pandava army during the war was Arjuna whose charioteer was Sri Krishna. Just before the war was t o begin, Arjuna requested Sri Krishna to take the chariot in the middle of the battlefield so that he could have a look at the warriors of the opposing armies. He was appalled by what he saw. Standing against each other were close relatives, friends, teachers and such others to kill and ready to get killed. This depressed him terribly, and he sunk into gloom and despair, 'O Krishna, my body quivers, mouth is parched, hairs stand on end, skin burns, head reels, body is soaked in sweat, and my bow slips from my hand…(I.30–31)'. Arjuna was drenched in tears at the prospect of unprecedented manslaughter, as a sorrowful person immersed in despair would be. He now wanted to give up everything and become a wandering monk.

Sri Krishna felt aghast at this development, since Arjuna had come prepared to take part in the war in accordance with his dharma, 'Wherefrom comes this lowness of spirit, unbecoming to an Aryan, dishonourable, an obstacle to the attaining of heaven? Yield not to unmanliness, Arjuna, it does not become you. Shake off this faint heartedness, and arise, O scorcher of enemies!' The idea was that one must not back out from one's duty during calamity. But the powerful words of the Lord had no effect on the great warrior. He sunk further in despair.

Sri Krishna then placed before Arjuna the philosophy of life, worldview, and spiritual truths to take him out of the mental crisis seeded by grief, delusion and sorrow. The aim of the Lord's teachings was to make Arjuna see things in proper perspective and thus make him conscious of his duties, *svadharma*, without imposing his own views on Arjuna. At the end of the talk Sri Krishna asked Arjuna to make his choice. By then the powerful discourse had removed the dark clouds of despondency from the minds of the great warrior, and he got up to take part in the war and win it.

The majestic calm of the teacher in the battlefield and his approach in solving a crisis situation, is simply unique. Instead of coaxing, inspiring, or ridiculing Arjuna into the war, Sri Krishna simply placed the philosophy of life before him, and showed that whatever outlook he might have towards life, he had to be consistent about it, which meant that he had to be true to his *svadharma*.

What Lord Krishna told Arjuna at that time, was versified by Vyasa in 700 shlokas, arranged in 18 chapters. Independently this is known as Gita, but it actually belongs to the *Bhishma Parva* (a section) of the *Mahabharata*. Thus Gita can be treated both as the words of the Lord, as is commonly believed, or can be treated as a work by Vyasa in which he presented the gist of the Vedas, and also harmonised the conflicting philosophies and religious outlooks of the period, as he had done in the parent work, *Mahabharata*. In either case Gita remains the most precious scripture of the Hindu race.

Even though an epical story, the strength oozing from the words of this small work is capable of pulling out anyone from the Charybdis of ultimate crisis, provided the person is willing to act according to the philosophy encapsulated in those words.

One naive allegation about Gita is that through his words Sri Krishna incited Arjuna for the war. But this is completely wrong. According to *Mahabharata*, when all peace process between Pandavas and Kauravas failed, only then the decision for the war was taken. And when Arjuna came prepared to fight, he had no right to back out from his sacred duty as per the conventions of *varnashrama dharma*. Sri Krishna only placed before Arjuna's vacilating mind the philosophy of life, and then asked him to make his own decision.

Content

Gita being the handbook of the Hindu religion, and the gist of all its scriptures, it is important to know what exactly it preaches, and what Hindu religion is about.

The goal of Gita is to preach dharma—the ways of life, in entirety. While every religion preaches one single path to God, Hinduism accepts innumerable paths to God that can be broadly classified into two, as presented in the Vedas. Of these, the first one is suitable for the householders, who are engaged in worldly duties, or are deep into action to achieve a goal. It is the religion for the doers, movers, shakers, and achievers. The second path is for the renunciates who give up the world and all worldly ties. These chosen ones do not have any duty, sacred or secular, left to perform. They go beyond desires and achievements, and if at all they work, it is for the welfare of others, without any self-interest.

These two paths are respectively known as *pravritti marg* (path of action), and *nivritti marg* (path of renunciation). This makes Gita a highly intense spiritual work that cannot be understood properly without commentaries and contemplation, even though its words are like music to ears, and easy to understand. No wonder there are thousands of commentaries, notes, explanations and interpretation on Gita—probably maximum in the world on a single book.

The goal of any book in the world is to teach what it considers good. The idea of goodness may differ, and may be acceptable to limited few, but the only goal of every book is to reveal what it considers right in the branch of knowledge that it discusses. The goal of Gita is to preach unto mankind the good, in fact, the highest good that makes a person an achiever in this world, and also helps one acquire superhuman strength to cut through the bonds of the world. Can there ever be a better good than this twin objective?

To cross the relative existence characterised by duality like birth and death, heat and cold, pleasure and pain, etc., one has to get rid of all worldly ties, including one's identification with one's body and mind and be established in the knowledge of divine oneness. When one practices divine oneness as sadhana (spiritual practice), there can never be any sense of duty, or a desire for action, since action presupposes duality. Hence, this path can be practised only by the few brave hearts with no self-interest left for this world and its affairs.

The second path is for those who want to be achievers. By nature people are lovers of action, and in many cases they end up being great doers. When one acts out of self-interest, they usually get worldly success, but when acts are performed as a matter of sacred duty, or without any selfish motive, or as an offering to the Lord, these lead to purification of mind and ultimately to self-knowledge. 'By performing action without attachment, one reaches the Supreme'.

Gita thus teaches complete detachment or unselfish action and also a complete surrender to God. In the process it describes God in its impersonal and personal aspects, along with the nature of self, creation, and self-knowledge.

Devotion to God is another important aspect that blooms in Gita. The Upanishads talk of *shraddha* (to love one's convictions) as an essential condition for spiritual growth, but this concept transforms into bhakti in Gita, and finds its fulfilment in the concept of *sharanagati* (self-surrender to God). In later times, the philosophy of self-surrender, reinforced by the Bhakti movement, became the major religious practice of the Hindus. The introduction of devotion as a core of spiritual practice in Gita made it a highly acceptable work—infinitely more than the Upanishads. This concept of surrender to God is to be found in the Puranas and elsewhere too, but because of the brevity of expression in Gita, it is easy to identify this outlook with this book more than anywhere else.

The great speciality of Gita lies in its synthetic character through which it harmonises the apparently opposing philosophies. Contradictions meet in Gita and get seamed into a whole, without compromising with the individuality of those contradictions. The Vedas had harmonised the Divine in its famous prayer, 'Truth is one, but sages call it variously', but different outlooks towards life and the philosophies emerging out of them were harmonised in Gita for the first time. One can thus feel the oneness of things and thoughts palpably in Gita.

Gita discusses life, world, and God at both micro and macro level, and thus show how the big is a fractal composed of the small. For example, it talks of action at cosmic level by which gods run the universe, and also as individual duty in the form of *varnashrama dharma*; rebirth is preached at the individual level, and the cyclic existence of the universe is explained at the macro level; God is the master of all, and as the *antaryamin* (the indwelling spirit), he is the master of the body; the universe is described as composed of the three basic qualities, *sattva, rajas, tamas* and an individual too is guided by these tendencies; the gods and demons are there at the cosmic level, while godly and demoniac propensities are present in every individual. There are many other such mentions. The philosophy behind this is that there is no minor or major differentiating chasm between the small and the big.

Perfection through Yogas

Each of the 18 chapters of Gita is named as a different yoga, which implies that a person can attain perfection by following any of these chapters. For example, the first chapter, *Arjuna Vishada Yoga*, meaning the yoga of Arjuna's sorrow, shows that one can get united with God even through sorrow, which indeed is true.

The purport of Gita is introduced in the first chapter. The second chapter lays out the subject matter of Gita in a short form. The next 15 chapters elaborate the ideas stated in the second chapter, and the last chapter sums up the philosophy and meaning of Gita, discussed in the previous chapters.

After giving a poetic description of Arjuna's confused mental state in the first chapter, the second chapter addresses the mental agony of Arjuna by way of Sri Krishna talking to him about the ultimate of Vedantic truth that man in essence is atman, 'It is neither born nor does it ever die; it does not come into being at some point of time, nor does it ever cease to exist. It is unborn, eternal, permanent, and primeval. So it does not get destroyed when the body is destroyed. How can a person who knows one's self as indestructible, eternal, unborn, and immutable think that he can kill someone or injure someone?' (II.20–21).

The philosophy behind this Upanishadic truth is simple—existence can never be non-existent. For example, take the statement, 'This is a pot'. Here two ideas work simultaneously in the mind—the idea of 'pot', and the idea of 'existence'. Now if that pot, or all the pots of the universe are destroyed, even then the idea of existence cannot be destroyed, since it will continue to be there through the presence of some other object. Even when one says that 'the pot does not exist', the idea of existence in the form of negation is invariably there the way it is said that 'he was conspicuous by his absence'. So, even if the entire creation is destroyed, the idea of 'existence' will continue to be there till there is any kind of awareness, positive or negative.

This argument has been mentioned here in brief, but it forms the most important argument base for Advaita Vedanta, and this has been elaborated, explained, and defended in innumerable treatise on Vedanta. Incidentally, truth (atman) as the only existence has been proclaimed by a large number of sages in Hinduism, and also in other religions. So more than a philosophical speculation, it is a spiritual truth.

This state of pure existence where there is nothing else other than sublime awareness is the true state of atman, which by its very nature cannot undergo any kind of existence, birth, growth, transformation, decay, or destruction. Death being a mere chimera, why would then a noble person give up one's dharma that brings to life all that is good and covetable, questioned the Lord. But as one can see, this highest philosophy of the Hindus is difficult to comprehend, and that is what happened with Arjuna too.

To persuade Arjuna not to give up his dharma (the core of *Mahabharata* philosophy), Sri Krishna then placed before him two additional outlooks current in India. The first one was that the embodied soul (not the all-pervading atman) continues to take up new bodies and give them up depending on the kind of action one has performed. So death and rebirth being certain, why should one give up one's dharma and invite sin on oneself?

The second outlook was that if life was a chance product of matter, as materialists think, then since one did not exist before one's birth a few years ago, and would cease to exist after a few years, why should one give up dharma and invite ridicule and slight till one was alive? Death being the cessation of everything for the individual, wasn't it better to have a glorious death than an ignominious one?

Thus Gita mentions three outlooks towards life, but its own philosophy lies with treating the individual as atman. According to it, a person is neither a product of matter, nor a product of spirit-matter duo, but he is the pure spirit, ever free, ever majestic. All power, all knowledge is inherent in him.

This knowledge of one's true nature can be attained directly only by giving up everything, but since not many are capable of doing so, Sri Krishna then talked about karma yoga, the path of action, which is the mainstay of the world, 'Work ceaselessly since that is your way of life, but never crave for its results if you want to be a yogi. A yogi works with all perfection, without suffering the agony of failure, or elation of success (II.47–48).' The idea is that one must neither seek, nor avoid if he wants to rise higher in life. Detachment, or in other words, unselfishness is the key to success in higher life. This demands equanimity of mind.

It is unfortunate that many misunderstand the philosophy of karma yoga, since it talks of detachment. Karma yoga emphasises that one has to work ceaselessly, paying perfect attention to every detail. Now if such a person does not succeed, who will? What this yoga adds is that since there are other factors behind the fructification of an act, one should not get into emotional swing by one's success or failure. Indeed, detachment (unselfishness) is the key to success, happiness, and fulfilment in life.

The last section of the second chapter discusses the nature of a person who is established in self-knowledge. The chief characteristic of such persons is that they never get swayed by emotions, nor do they get involved in any kind of worldly pleasures, 'When a man dwells on the thought of an object, he feels attached to it. This gives rise to desire, which when not fulfilled leads to anger. Anger leads to clouding of mind that impairs judgement. This ultimately results in utter ruin (II.62–3).' To avoid such degradation, the wise never allow their mind to see the beautiful or the avoidable of the world.

The third chapter describes the nuances of karma yoga, according to which one has to work consciously, either for oneself or for the welfare of others, since action is embedded in creation. No created being can live without activity even for a moment, but to be a yogi one has to practise unselfishness. Lord emphasises the point, 'I have no duty; there is nothing that I have not gained, and nothing that I have to gain; even then I continue to work...for, if I do not work, these worlds would perish...(III.22–4).' This is the idea behind unselfishness: one has to work like a master, and not like a servant. Only then karma yoga can be performed.

In contrast, the fourth chapter is dedicated to the way of knowledge, according to which one has to strive to gain the knowledge of God by treating all one's actions as yajna, and all its accessories as Brahman, the supreme reality, 'To him the instrument of offering is Brahman, the offered object, the fire in which offering is made, the performer, the act, as also the result—all are Brahman'. To a knower of Brahman, there is nothing other than Brahman, and hence he indeed sees things thus. This is true of the devotees too who see God everywhere.

In Hindu spirituality, the goal and the way are treated as non-different. Normally a work produces results that are different from the act. For example, one eats to satisfy one's hunger, implying that the act and the result are different. Similarly when one worships God to gain some result, the cause and effect are different. But at the higher levels of spirituality, the goal and the way are one and the same. For example, if a person is devoted to God, he would like to see God everywhere, and for that he has to start seeing God everywhere. Similarly, if a person wants to attain self-knowledge, then he has to practise seeing the divine non-difference all the time. It means that one has to practise even the most trivial acts like eating, breathing, reading, charity, etc. as yajna in which every accessory is Brahman, the supreme non-dual reality. Thus when a person makes a gift, he has to think of the gift, the receiver, the act, himself, and the result of it—everything as Brahman. A mind blowing reality! The resulting self-knowledge burns down every kind of duality—virtue-vice, life-death, good-bad, etc.

The fourth chapter is also famous for its verse on God's incarnating powers, 'Whenever there is a decline of dharma, and a rise of adharma, I incarnate for the protection of the good, for the destruction of the wicked, and for the establishment of the dharma. (IV.7–8)'. This outlook is in consonance with the idea of God incarnating in different age, and in different body to stabilise the world order.

The fifth chapter extols the philosophy of sannyasa, according to which one has to master the universe by gaining the knowledge of self here and now. This can be done by overcoming the dualities that plague the internal and external existence.

The sixth chapter is devoted to the practice of yoga by controlling one's inner and external organs, which is essential for the attainment of knowledge of the self. The control over senses and sense organs lead to the control of mind, which ultimately leads to self-knowledge in due course. A yogi who does not succeed in one life need not despair, since he is reborn in a noble family, from where he takes up to his way of yoga again, after working out his bad karma.

The seventh to twelfth chapter describes the nature of God and his loving relation with the world. Phenomenal in its philosophical content, poetic beauty, and marvellous harmonising of the micro and the macro, this section is a must read for all those who have devotional tendencies.

God of Gita, and consequently of Hinduism, is qualitatively different from God of every other religion. He is neither transcendent, nor immanent, nor a combination of these. 'I (God) pervade all things, all beings exist in me, but I do not exist in them. And yet the beings do not dwell in me—that is my divine mystery. My spirit, which is the support of all things, does not dwell in them (IX.4-5)'. It means that the Lord is neither the container nor the contained, since there is no duality in him. In truth, he is above all cause-effect relationship, and in the ultimate analysis, the subject and object are same, but in the relative world he appears to be the creator and the indwelling spirit of all. There is no false God in the universe since 'even those who worship any deity with faith, they too worship me (IX.23).'

God is all that is there in the world. He is the sacred of the world like Ganga, Aum, Gayatri, etc., and is the powerful like Rama, and is also the vicious death. Not only that, he is also the gambling among cheats, and silence among the secretive! (X).

The finale comes when the Lord reveals his *Virat* (the cosmic) form to Arjuna (XI) wherein he is seen to be pervading the entire universe, and in whom all beings are present. Arjuna prayed to that form, 'I behold thee as one without beginning, middle, or end, with infinite arms and immeasurable strength; with the sun and moon as thine eyes…by thou alone are filled all the space… and the three world tremble with fear…beholding thy great form, with myriads of mouths, eyes, arms, thighs, feet, and bellies—the worlds are terrified…All these warrior from both sides are entering Your tusked and terrible mouths, frightful to behold. Some are seen caught between thy teeth, their heads crushed to powder…As moths rush into a blazing fire to perish, so do all these are rushing into thy mouth. Thou lickest thy lips, and thou are devouring all the worlds on every side with thy flaming mouths. The fiery rays fill the whole universe.' And to think that both the armies were yet to begin the war. The true conviction that God alone is true, comes to a person only after he has experienced such a vision.

Chapters 13 to 17 discuss the nature of the world in relation to God. The focus is to cut at the root of one's worldly existence by first becoming active, then noble, and then going beyond both good and bad. This is known as cutting the roots of the world, and this alone is the goal of life. In chapter 15 the world is compared to an *asvattha* tree whose roots and branches are spread everywhere, and this has to be cut down by the discriminatory axe and prayers to God.

This section also discusses the nature of consciousness and its effect on matter. Everything that one experiences in the universe belongs to the empire of matter and hence must be shunned to be established in the freedom of spirit. Those who strive to give up the products of matter, are the people with divine tendencies, while those who wish to acquire more and more, are the demonic types. Religion and spirituality is meant only for those who have godly nature, says Gita.

Chapter 18 gathers the spread that was there in the previous chapters and ends with, 'Give up all dharma (good and bad acts), and seek shelter in me. Rest assured, I will take you out of all sins (good and bad are both treated as sin in spirituality since these both bind a person to the world), and set you free (from the relative existence) (XVIII.66).

What has been offered here is just a glimpse of this precious scripture, since it is impossible to detail its content in such a short paper.

Relevance in Present Times

Over thousands of years, Gita has come to be treated as the spiritual and philosophical heartbeat of India. Every Hindu lives and dreams in Gita, and when he dies, he is given a farewell of chants from Gita. Every practising Hindu makes it a point to recite from it daily, every philosophical Hindu tries to study and understand the work, and every mystic Hindu strives to mould his life according to Gita. Who knows? Probably the future Hindus may accept only Gita as its scripture.

The best that India has to give to the world in the fields of wisdom, religion, philosophy and spirituality is Gita—the precious scripture.

Supporting Scriptures

TANTRA–SMRITI

This section discusses two important classes of sacred books, Tantra and Smriti, which even though do not belong to the mainstream scriptures, have come to fill up the gaps that a Hindu may find while practising a religious life. The sacred books discussed till now detail things. This approach of detailing everything does help the less evolved, but in the long run these degenerate into creating a social wrap for the followers.

There are a lot many things in religion that need continuous update. Hindu religion does not want these updates, or even the gaps to be worked by one's own skewed understanding, coloured by self-interest. Tantra and Smriti did that job.

TANTRA

The preceding sections on the primary scriptures reveal how the Hindu race has come to perceive God both as impersonal and personal. More importantly, they believe that in his personal aspect God can manifest his power in any form. The manifestation of God's power, including the creation of universe, is never an act, as the term is commonly used, rather it is effected by his mere will, since God's will and its actualisation are same. God being pure consciousness, he is the repository of all strength, and hence he does not have to act through mind, senses, organs, and objects to materialise his will the way we have to do.

What might then happen if the Lord ever thinks of himself as feminine? God being beyond the cause-effect phenomena, only a naive can define God as being mere this or that. God being infinite and pure consciousness, he can have a particular form, and also many other forms simultaneously, along with being formless. That is the true meaning of being infinite. If he thinks of himself as a boar or fish, who can stop him from manifesting in those forms, since his thinking and act are same.

There being no second—superior or inferior—to him, he may very well think of himself (rather itself) as feminine too. After all, gender is a dividing characteristic of dualistic existence that can never apply to God. Tantra and Shakti worships are rooted in this concept of seeing the Divine as feminine.

It was mentioned in the section on the Puranas how the idea of Mother worship comes from the Vedas, and how the Puranas elaborated them. The real growth of Mother worship in India probably came from the Tantra traditions that influenced even the Puranas, since these are the scriptural behemoths that consume everything that comes its way. In the present-day Hinduism, Mother worship mostly comes from the Puranic traditions, but their roots, and the mantras used in them have clear footprints of Tantra.

Independent of the Puranic traditions, Tantras produced great sages who popularised it in certain sections of the society, but due to many reasons, Tantra practices could not be accepted, appreciated, and absorbed in the mainstream Hinduism. One chief reason for it was that unlike the Vedic systems, Tantras are highly esoteric, meaning that their practices are secret, and also that their texts have layered meanings, and hence these cannot be understood unless a teacher trained in Tantra traditions explains them. This kind of closed system is always dangerous for the practitioners and the onlookers alike. Be it a secretive person, a secret society, or a secret branch of knowledge—these can never be relied upon fully. The same happened with the Tantras—its esoteric nature made the spiritually cultured wary of it, and so it thrived mostly in the darkness of secrecy without the benefits of corrective adjustments that comes to an open system. However, the contribution of Tantras to Mother worship cannot be undermined.

Here it is important to remember that religions, religious systems, and their outlooks are never a thought-out system the way most philosophies are. Religions are the externals around the spiritual truths concerning God—the way he is, and the way he is perceived by the great sages in the depths of their meditation. A thought-out religion like Akbar's Din e-Ilahi, or Humanism are put to the bins of history faster than it took them to be gestated, and the truths represented by them are as replaceable as a man's clothes. But it is not so with religions that have withstood the test of time. The applications of the truths represented by them may be skewed, and the rationale to explain them may be flawed, but the spiritual truths that they represent cannot be questioned.

The principle behind Shakti/Mother worship is that God creates the universe through his power which is non-different from him, the way fire and its burning power are one and the same. This power of God is known as *shakti*, which is non-different from God, and hence worshipping it is same as worshipping God.

Philosophically speaking, when God is in non-creative mode, he alone exists. At that time his *shakti* stays merged in him. But when he wills to manifest his power, it appears as his creation. How and why God wills so, is a divine mystery that no religion can ever answer satisfactorily, since the dividing line of Mind-Time-Space separates the absolute from the relative. This dividing line is called variously by different schools of philosophy. The *vedantins* call it maya, devotees call it divine play, while Shakti worshippers call it Shakti. The branching out of different philosophies in Hinduism is mostly due to their difference in perception of this dividing line between the absolute and the relative.

Creation by God is effected through Shakti. The difference between any two beings lies in the manifestation of Shakti in them, and even incarnations of God belong to the realm of Shakti, since their divine play is carried out in this world—the area of Shakti.

Mahanirvan Tantra, an important work on Tantra describes Shakti as,

> Thou art the supreme power of Brahman, and from thee has sprung the whole universe. You are its Mother. Whatever there is in this world, with or without motion, owes its origin to thee, and is dependent on thee. Thou art the origin of all the manifestations; thou art the birthplace of even us (Brahma, Vishnu, Shiva). Thou knowest the whole world, yet none know thee. (*Mahananirvan Tantra*, 4.10–12)

This gives a fair idea about what Shakti worship is about. Of these Shakti worshippers, most prefer to address it as Mother due to the love and sweetness associated with one's mother that can be felt at the cosmic level too.

Origin

Tantras grew independent of the Vedic traditions, and may have come earlier to it. The occasional mention of certain rites and rituals in scriptures hint at Tantra's antiquity, but it never grew as a cohesive religion the way the Vedas grew. Tantra drew from different practices current in India like Shaivism, and its philosophy came mostly from Samkhya (to be discussed in the section on philosophy). Later, some schools of Buddhism amalgamated their philosophy with Tantra to develop Vajrayana school of Buddhism. This school became popular in Tibet and later it entered India in its new avatar. The present-day Tantra is thus a mix of Hindu and Buddhist traditions of Tantra rituals.

The later Tantric texts like *Mahanirvan Tantra* wanted to connect their doctrines with the Vedas but the orthodox Vedic tradition did not allow the proximity, even though both systems have much in common. For example, both systems preach common goals of life (dharma, artha, etc.); the Vedas are concerned with the victory of man over the forces of nature while in the Tantric sadhana also the chief concern is the ascendancy of man over nature, both external and internal; the offering of *Soma rasa* was replaced by wine in the Tantras; and, the animal sacrifice of the Vedas became an essential ritual in the Tantra. But the Vedic traditions being all powerful in Hindu religion, Tantras had to remain satisfied with being on the sidelines even though it contributed significantly in its rites, rituals, and modes of worship.

In spite of the slight faced by the Vedic tradition, Tantra grew partly due to the failure of the Vedic system in the changed times, and partly because it offered quick-fix solutions to the need and greed of common man. The requirements for Vedic rituals had become impractical—the ingredients used in Vedic sacrifices were too difficult to obtain, the lifestyle prescribed for a practitioner became nearly impossible to follow, and the promised results of heavens after death seemed too distant. On the other hand, the Upanishadic meditations were too difficult for a common man to follow, and the Puranas appeared as tales of fantasy. But the devout needed something concrete, something simpler, and something glamorous for them to acquire worldly good and to destroy their ill wishers. The answer was Tantra.

Texts and Traditions

Classified broadly, there are three types of Tantra texts—Agama, Yamala, and Buddhistic texts. According to the traditions, Tantra is believed to have been taught by the great Lord Shiva to Parvati, his divine consort, the Shakti. This kind of texts are called Agama. There are also texts in which Parvati instructs Lord Shiva in the art of Tantras. These are called Nigama. However, collectively all these texts are known as Agama.

Another class of literature are known as Yamala. These are eight in number and have the tradition of Bhairava, instead of the Lord Shiva. The most famous work of this group is *Brahma Yamala*. Yamalas indicate a great development in the Tantric sadhana that give a well-developed mode of worship, harmonise a lot of local deities and cults, make provision for sadhana by people of all castes, and introduce a great variety of gods and goddesses. The major shift in these works, as compared to the Agama literature is the worship of Shakti instead of Lord Shiva.

The Buddhistic traditions of Tantra had mainly three forms— Vajrayana, Sahajayana, and Kalachakrayana. The philosophical basis for these works was supplied by the Yogachara and the Madhyamika systems of Buddhistic philosophy. Vajrayana emphasises the importance of mantra (repetition of sacred mantras), *mudra* (certain bodily positions), and *mandala* (schematic representation of mystic powers); Sahajayana discards all formalism; and Kalachakrayana attaches importance to *muhurta, tithi, nakshtra,* etc., thus bringing the elements of astrology and astronomy in sadhana.

Geographically, there are four classes of Tantra: Kerala, Kashmira, Gauda, and Vilas, but their influence is not really confined to one region. With time they spread all over the country and got intertwined with each other. Thus Tantra traditions have been widespread throughout the country in various forms, made famous by personalities like Matsyendranath, Gorakhnath, Siddhacharya, and others. Of the sects, Kaula, Natha, and Avadhuta have been more popular. In Bengal, Vaishnava Sahjiya sect has been popular that treats Radha as Shakti, and Krishna as the supreme reality. This sect later gave birth to the popular sect of Bauls.

It is difficult to give an overview of all these sects and their mode of sadhana. However, it is important to note that the ignorance of the general public and the abuse by the irresponsible practitioners of Vamachara or 'left-hand' path of Tantra, has made the Tantras a big suspect in the eyes of many. The ritual of this path is based upon the principle of the 'return current', which seeks to reverse the process by which a man tends to become like an animal. The goal is to slowly raise the animal-man to the Divine through his victory over the five pleasurable elements of life, known as the five 'M', *pancha makara—mansa, matsya, madya, mudra, maithuna—* meat, fish, wine, fried cereals, and union. The underlying principle of Vamachara is to emphasise the fact that a man makes progress in spiritual life not by falsely shunning that which makes him fall, but by seizing upon it and sublimating it so as to make it a means of liberation.

Mahanirvan Tantra, an important work on Tantra, explains the five 'M' as being representative of the five great elements of nature. According to it, wine represents fire element, fish represents water element, meat represents air element, fried grains represent earth element, and union is the representative of the ether (*akasa*) element. By offering these to the Mother of the universe, one worships her through her own creative elements.

Hinduism accepts the sacred, but never the secret. So the secrecy and socially unacceptable practices associated with Tantra sadhana that were carried out in cremation grounds, lonely places, and forests with the aid of females, wine, skulls, etc. fascinated some, but was abhorred by the most. So in spite of promises of big rewards in this world and the next for the Tantra practitioners, the system could not become popular.

Content

The Tantras admit the validity of the rituals of the Vedas, the discrimination and renunciation of the Upanishads, the purifying disciplines of yoga, and the passionate love for the deity described in the Puranas. They exhort the aspirants to exercise will and self-effort, practise self-surrender, and supplicate for divine grace. Tantras promise their followers not only enjoyment of worldly happiness but also liberation (*bhoga* and *apavarga*). The system acknowledges that the power of the kundalini (mystic power inherent in all) can be aroused by the sincere pursuit of any spiritual discipline, and that this arousal can bring infinite achievement.

As with the Vedas, Tantra too accepts Satchidananda— Existence–Knowledge–Bliss as the supreme reality that manifests the creation, which is significantly different from the nature of God. According to the Vedanta philosophy, this difference is apparent, known as maya, that exists only on the relative plane at the time of creation, preservation, and destruction. In truth God alone exists, always, all the time. According to them, neither the creation is ultimately real, nor are created beings real. True knowledge, acquired in the deeper states of intuitive wisdom, known as samadhi, reveals only an undifferentiated consciousness.

According to Tantra, however, Satchidananda is called Shiva-Shakti. The hyphenated word suggests that Shiva or the absolute, and Shakti (Lord's power), are eternally conjoined like a word and its meaning; and that the one cannot be thought of without the other. According to Tantra, the concept of pure consciousness which denies Shakti is only half of the truth. Satchidananda is essentially endowed with the power of self-evolution and self-involution. Therefore perfect spiritual knowledge is the knowledge of the whole: of consciousness as 'being' and consciousness as power 'to become'.

When the creation takes place, the absolute become relative, and then Shiva and Shakti appear as separate entities, although they are not so in reality. The worship of Shiva and Shakti, as performed in Hinduism, is indicative of their interplay that effects the creation. This way both creation and the individual soul (*jiva*) are treated as real in Tantra. It may be remembered here that according to Advaita Vedanta both *jiva* and creation are the play of name and form upon Brahman.

According to Tantra, the non-dual reality becomes evolved, which is real and not merely apparent as in Vedanta. This evolution gives certain kind of powers and also restricts every form of existence (starting from a stone to human beings). This accounts for a being's actions and reactions. These determinants are the 'fetters' (*pasa*), which weave the whole fabric of the *jiva*'s phenomenal life.

164

It is by them that one gets bound and behaves like an animal (*pasu*). The goal of Tantra is to teach the method by which these bondages can be cut asunder to make every *jiva* one with Shiva.

This outlook separates Tantra from Visishtadvaita and *Dvaita*, since neither of these schools accepts the oneness of the individual with the universal. Thus the philosophy of Tantra takes the elements of all the three main branches of Vedanta, and is yet separate from each one of them.

When a *sadhaka* attains the purity of mind through the ritualistic worship as prescribed in the Tantras, he becomes fit for the realisation of Brahman. It is then that an aspirant finds that the meditator, meditation, and the object of meditation are all one.

Tantra as a Mode of Sadhana

Tantras, along with the Puranas, have contributed hugely in the present day rituals of Hinduism. Some of these are mentioned here.

Mantras: These play an important part in the Tantras. The word literally means 'that which, when reflected upon, gives liberation'.

It was explained in the section on the Upanishads how Aum is the sound equivalent of God. Tantra takes this concept one step forward with the idea that every deity, including Mother and Shakti are aspects of consciousness that appears in three forms—sound equivalent, geometric equivalent, and physical manifestation. The mantras are the sound equivalent of deity for which it is intended. By repeating a mantra and meditating on its meaning, an aspirant is believed to get the vision of its physical manifestation.

Tantra regards vibration as a manifestation of the cosmic energy or Shakti and teaches that proper vibration can lead to the deity from which it emanates, the way radio works on different wavelengths. Mantras are thus treated as forms of concentrated thought of exceeding potency.

The mantras are also classified as masculine, feminine and neuter. Masculine mantras end in *hum* and *phat*; feminine mantras end in *swaha*, and neuter mantras end in *namah*.

Beeja (lit. seed): These play an important role in the Tantras. Just like Aum of the Vedas, these *beeja* are mystic sounds produced by the combination of various sounds. There are innumerable *beeja*, but the more popular ones are *aim* (worship of Saraswati), *hrim* (worship of Shakti), *shrim* (worship of Lakshmi). Some of these *beejas* are masculine (eg. *klim*, denoting the God of desire), while most of them are feminine. Most mantras given by a spiritual teacher in India have *beeja* in them.

Yantras: Mystical diagrams called 'yantras' are the diagrammatic (geometric) equivalent of the deity, just as mantra is its sound-equivalent. Being non-different from the deity that it represents, a yantra is representation of the power represented by the deity. For example, the popular Sri yantra, used in the worship of Goddess Durga and other shakti, is formed by nine interlocking triangles radiating from a central point. The drawing of this yantra is accepted as having Mother and all her powers manifest in it. Thus yantra and mantra are fundamentally same. According to Tantras, mantras are efficacious, yantras are potent, and the deities represented by them are verily present during worship, if it is done properly.

Kundalini: The spiritual awakening of a sadhaka is described in Tantra by means of the kundalini power. The idea of kundalini has permeated Hindu spiritual thoughts deeply. Every genuine spiritual experience, such as the seeing of light or a vision, or communion with the deity, is a manifestation of the awakening and ascent of the kundalini.

Kundalini is the infinite energy in potential form in every being that releases only a very small amount of working energy for one's daily life. The coiled up kundalini is the pivot upon which the complex apparatus of the body and mind moves and turns. Once the kundalini is aroused, the potential gets converted into the kinetic, like the release of energy from a huge reservoir or as during an atomic explosion.

The release of this power, through Tantra sadhana, or by other means like concentration, results in both worldly success, and also in spiritual attainments, depending on the desire of the concerned person. When the latent energy is released in full, an aspirant breaks all fetters that chain him to the worldly existence, and he merges with the supreme consciousness, God.

Chakras: Tantra practices believe that there are seven centres of consciousness, known as chakra, in every person. The first three, known as Muladhara, are the base centres in the lower part of the body. The kundalini stays coiled up there like a snake holding its tail in its mouth. The remaining four chakras are respectively in the heart, throat, between the eyebrows, and the head.

The passage of the awakened kundalini lies through a nerve centre, *sushumana,* that normally remains closed for the common person. When the consciousness of a person is awakened, the kundalini (or, the centre of consciousness) passes through Sushumna in which each chakra looks like a different coloured lotus with varying numbers of petals. In the case of an ordinary person, these centres (chakras) are closed, and the lotuses droop down like buds. But as the kundalini rises through the Sushumna and touches the centres, these buds turn upward as fully opened flowers and the aspirant obtains spiritual experiences, along with the indomitable power that is seen in spiritual persons.

Rituals

Rituals are the crystallised philosophy of any system, religious or social. It is through rituals, ceremonies, anniversaries, and festivals that an individual remains tied with one's society. It is through these that a student feels close with one's institution, and a military person identifies himself with his regiment and the country. Take away ritual from a person's life, and they would feel shut out, and may also become wayward.

Many a couple fight only because the partner might have forgotten to observe the ritual of celebrating some anniversary. This is true with religious followers too. Rituals make one grow in commitment, but these also keep one tied to the religion. Look at any religion, and it would be seen how mechanical people can be when it comes to religious drills. Hinduism is no exception. It prescribes philosophy for the evolved minds, and advocates rituals and recitals for the less advanced.

Hindu rituals are a combination of Puranic and Tantra traditions. The most common ritual or puja is performed at home or at some temple in front of some image, idol, or some symbol like Shivalinga. Wherever Tantra traditions are followed, there yantra is also used, in addition to mantras and rituals associated with them.

The images and idols used during worship represent some aspect of the Divine. The practitioners either visualise the deities present within themselves, or try to feel their presence outside. In the external worship, the deities are usually worshipped with flowers, incense, and other offerings, or as the local practice may demand. In addition, one need ablutions (*snana*) for physical purity, *tarpana* for inner satisfaction, *bhutasuddhi* to frees oneself of taints, and *dhyana* enables the worshipper to feel his oneness with the deity.

Tantra in Present Times

The West has suddenly woken up to the charms of Tantra for all the dirty reasons, as it has lapped up yoga for its aerobics. The re-entry of Tantra from abroad makes it appear more suspicious than it was in earlier times. However, in spite of the blemishes that it has, and the neglect that it had to face due to this, it has served Hinduism well through its contribution in the areas of rituals and simplification of certain kinds of spiritual practices.

The concept of transference by which a person overcomes his base nature to become divine by using the objects of pleasure, is unique in the history of world religions. It is this transference, or sublimation that made a large many ordinary minds attain some upliftment. It was through Tantra that people learnt that instead of killing animals for pleasure, one may sacrifice it and then consume it in moderate quantities. This way one indulges in a measured way.

Sri Ramakrishna, the great unifier of Hinduism, practised various kinds of Tantra sadhana to vet them for their correctness. He, however, did not approve of many of its practices, which fortunately has faded away from the general consciousness in the present times. On the other hand, he repeatedly talked about the importance of awakening of kundalini as a mark of spiritual progress, thus giving credence to certain doctrines of Tantra.

It all implies that Tantras are here to stay. May be in a more refined form.

SMRITI

The desire to live and continue living, whether in physical body, on some other plane, with God, or as atman, is common with every human being. In most cases this desire extends beyond one's body to encompass all those whom one loves. This gives rise to philosophy of existence that can be categorised in two broad forms—'live and let die' and 'live and let live'. Of these, the first one is driven by instinct and the second one is regulated by codes of conduct that is imposed on an individual by the society. These codes may have come through consensus, by order of the powerful, or by divine command. Whatever the origin of such codes, the goal of every such regulatory command is to suppress the savage nature of a person and make him a gentleman, superman, or divine.

The most famous code of conduct from ancient times is the code of Hammurabi (c. 1760 BCE) from Mesopotamia, which was based on the principle of 'an eye for an eye' and 'an arm for an arm'. Religious lawgivers have been more liberal that way. Laws given by Moses, more popularly known as Ten Commandments, has played an important role in the Judeo-Christian traditions that made them rise above tribal culture, and the laws given by Buddha, and Zarathustra have made their followers tolerant, mild, and good natured.

Smritis are the law books of the Hindu race. These are, however, neither mere law books, nor are they like the constitution of a country, or of an organised society. These are not even commandments, but are shastras, scriptures. Shastra means 'that which governs', and is applied to a book only if it teaches the ways and means to live in this world, as also show the path to attain mukti—liberation. In the process, these describe the nitty-gritty of morality, ethics, conduct, mores, justice, punishment, etc. by explaining the *vidhi* (what one should do) and *nisedha* (what one must not do) to attain the four aims of life—*dharma, artha, kama, moksha*. Smritis are thus scriptures that go beyond the parameters of law books of every other kind.

Origin

It was mentioned in the earlier sections how the Vedas are the fountainhead of Hindu religion from which nearly every branch of knowledge prevalent in India has flown out. The Vedas dealt mostly with yajna. To help the Vedic priests perform various details connected with a sacrifice, a kind of manual was worked out. With time each Veda had its own handbook of rituals written in a short form (sutra), or in metrical form. These came to be known as Kalpa that contained details regarding sacrifices, both public and private. With time, more specialised literature, known as Dharma Sutras came into existence that dealt exclusively with dharma, which is defined as right, duty, law, religion, custom, and usage. Most of the Dharma Sutras originated in the Vedic schools, but some of them like *Gautama Dharma Shastra*, and *Manusmriti* are independent works, although rooted in the Vedic tradition.

The Vedas are accepted as words of God channelled through the realisations of the sages, while Smritis were written by sages. Unlike other law books, or commandments, Smritis were codification of what was being practised in the society by the majority of people of that period. It was obvious to the sages that to make the society run smoothly, it was necessary for all the members to follow a common code of conduct. So, whenever the society changed its habits and behaviour pattern due to changed circumstances, the sages noted them, and then codified them without going against the spiritual principles of the Vedas. The wisdom and saintliness of the sage who wrote a particular Smriti added value to it, and helped it acquire popularity.

The aim of each of these Smritis is only one—how to help a person evolve spiritually so that one can attain the best in this life and in the next. Smritis do give importance to the society, but individuals are more important in them. This is a major departure in the outlook of the Smritis in comparison to the Western law books, or even the Indian Constitution. In these law books of modern times, society gets more importance than the growth of an individual.

Smritis are suggestive in nature, and hence these are not binding on anyone, the way other law books are. Due to this, Smritis are also known as *Suhrit Samhita*, meaning 'friendly advice'. Kings and societies used these Smritis as the guiding principle, without being dictated by it. The real governance was in the hands of the kings who, in spite of their power, went by one of these law books.

Because of their human origin, Smritis, as a class, are dynamic and subject to regular updates and amendments, depending on the changes in the society. For example, in matters of food, the climatic availability and other factors make it necessary to change the rules that govern them. So, one finds certain prohibitions in one Smriti, while that prohibition may not be there in some other. This applies to every other habit and practices of the Hindu society. So, great lawgivers amended the existing laws from time to time. They made alterations, adaptations, readjustments, additions, and deletions to suit the needs of the time so that a person could live his life in accordance with the Vedic ideals, despite the changed conditions.

Content

There are 18 main Smritis or Dharma Shastras of which *Manusmriti*—the law by Manu is the most celebrated because of its catholicity, rationality, and antiquity. Next in importance are the Smritis by Yajnavalkya and Parasara. In addition to these, there are innumerable Smritis current in different parts of the country.

Castes, Communities, and Individual

Whenever one thinks of Hinduism, the first thing to come to mind is its much maligned caste system. It is not known for sure how it came into existence, and then how it calcified into unbreakable moulds over thousands of years. It finds mention in the Vedas and *Ramayana* that shows its antiquity. By the time of *Mahabharata*, the caste system had made its permanent residence in the Hindu society. It is only in recent times that the seemingly unbreakable moulds of castes have started showing signs of crumbling.

The caste system has its origin possibly in the jati (guild) that was common in India since ancient times. Every society has trade guilds that take care of its members. In India, these guilds were known as jati (lit. related to birth), that explained the work performed by them. Although technically a guild, jati got hooked with family trade that every member was expected to join. A jati was not truly hidebound, since there are innumerable examples when a person gave up the occupation of his family to take up something different. For example, Drona and Parashuram were from Brahmin caste but became warriors, whereas Viswamitra was from warrior caste but became a Brahmin. However, the general practice was to hold on to one's jati because of ease of learning the trade and protection of the individual by the guild associated with it.

These guilds came to be classified into four varnas (caste)— Brahmin, Kshatriya, Vaishya, Shudra—who respectively became the custodians of the society's learning, safety, wealth, and service. The guiding principle of these four classes was that by staying true to one's duties without any self-interest, one could attain the four goals of life. The hierarchy of these varnas was based on the quantum of sacrifice that they were expected to make to be true to their duty. In return, the only privilege they got was relatively more respect. Thus Brahmins got maximum respect because as a caste they were expected to sacrifice their life and luxuries for learning. Compared to them, Kshatriyas got less respect because they could indulge in luxuries, but had to make sacrifice of their life, if so demanded, in a war. Similarly a monk got unconditional and universal highest respect because he gave up everything—even the desire to live or die.

In later times, the higher castes held on to their privileges but compromised with their duties in the sense that they became self-centred. This pushed the lowest class into abject poverty and abysmal ignorance.

There was a fifth class, known as Chandala, who were outcastes of the society. They did not have any privilege, nor were they expected to make any sacrifice. But being outcastes, they were not allowed any interaction with the caste people, which meant that they had a near animal like existence. The cruelty inflicted by the higher castes on them by way of shutting them out from every possible means of cultural evolution was abominable. In the long run, Hinduism had to pay a very heavy price for neglecting its masses—Shudras and Chandala.

Along with the four varna, there were four ashrama (stations of life)—Brahmacharya (student days), Grihastha (householder), Vanaprastha (reticent), and Sannyasa (monkhood). It was expected that every individual would live a life of dignity and meaning according to the stage in which he was. Thus, an elderly man was expected to give up everything to his children and leave his home permanently to spend the remaining years in the contemplation of God. However, unlike the varna, ashrama was not followed rigorously.

The duty of a person (*svadharma*) was determined by his varna and ashrama, and was popularly known as *varnashrama dharma* that comprised of six duties: *varna dharma* (general caste duties), *ashrama dharma* (general duties related to the station of life), *varnashrma dharma* (based on the particular station of a particular caste), *nimitta dharma* (penances), *guna dharma* (duties born of a particular position, e.g. that of a king), and *samanya* (duties common to all). For thousands of years, Hindus have followed their *svadharma* to attain the four goals of life. In Gita too, Sri Krishna taught Arjuna the importance of *svadharma*, going to the extent of telling that 'it was better to die carrying out one's duty than to switch over to others'.

Svadharma

Smritis specialise in defining *svadharma*—the duty of a person in relation to everything in the world. The focus in each of these books is on the individual's growth through the performance of one's duties, instead of merely making sacrifices for others, as any ethical system or a constitution demands. Altruism for the sake of altruism does not find favours in the Smritis, as also octane-filled words like 'ask not what your country can do for you, ask what you can do for your country', etc. are out of bounds in Smritis. To them, a person is the centre of his existence, and hence care has to be taken for his journey from being individual to becoming universal.

In matters of sacrificing, a person was expected to sacrifice the interests of the smaller group for the larger. Thus an individual should be sacrificed in the interest of the family, a family for a village, a village for a district, and a district for a state. Interestingly,

Manu says that one must sacrifice everything to acquire self-knowledge! This goes on to show how much importance Manu gives to the individual over the collective.

Purity of Purpose

There comes situation in life when even the greats tend to get swayed by their emotions. For those aspiring for spiritual upliftment, the control of mind is essential, and hence it is imperative that they live strictly according to values and ethics. Since Smritis lay down broad principles that help people make choice in such conflict situation where base emotions try to take over the intellect, and make the mind gross, it was important for people to follow the Smriti of their land and period.

Unlike the utopian ideas of equality of all men, Hinduism in general, and Smritis in particular treat inequality, both at individual and at the community level, as a fact of life. This inequality is most stark at the mental level that expresses itself in the form of ideals and aspirations of people that range from crass materialism of acquisition for oneself to the rarefied ideals of giving up everything.

Smritis being scriptures, these preach the ideal of a person's divine nature. The acquired materialism that one sees all around can go away only by giving up, since the defects are acquired, and not inherent. So, the guiding principle behind every Smriti, law, code, etc. is unselfishness. 'Give up,' these books say in every page and every instruction; he who gives up more is refined and culture, and he who holds on to the world has to be gently led through stages of evolution till he becomes fit to give up all to be established in his divine nature.

Like individuals, communities too are ranged between the Chandala way of life at one end, and the exalted ideals of Brahminical values that lead to spiritual realisation on the other. The goal of

Smritis is to take every community from being self-centred and steeped in bodily pleasures to being learned, cultured and evolved. What the Smritis wish the individuals to be, they also wish for a community, i.e. to be established in the culture of 'giving up'. As a community frees itself from the shackles of the body, it moves towards the culture of learning, wisdom and spirituality from being self-centred and mired in bodily pleasures.

Smritis did not treat the limitations of men, or of a community to be fundamental, or even presumable. One finds in *Mahabharata* and in other Smritis the outlook that if a Shudra has noble qualities then he is to be treated as a Brahmin, and that if the Shudras take up the manner and customs of the Brahmins they should be encouraged.

Absoluteness of Law of Karma

Like the acceptance of *svadharma* rooted in *varnashrama*, Smritis believe strongly in the laws of karma, according to which good or bad that comes in one's life is due to one's own past actions. Once a person accepts the law of karma to be true, he comes to realise the importance of his own freedom to regulate his conduct by rational volitions and power to conquer his impulses. It is then that he needs the help of scriptural guidelines that would help him come out of his lusting for the world to yearning for the spirit.

Unfortunately, the conviction in the absoluteness of law of karma was to be the nemesis of the Smritis. Instead of believing that one can improve one's lot by being good, the emphasis shifted to condemning the poor and the lower-caste people by bringing in the argument that they were wretched because they had done wrong in the past. Smritis nowhere talk like this, but the general belief turned towards that, alienating the masses from the mainstream.

Smritis deal with topics that can be classified as: *achara* (rites), *vyavahara* (dealings), and *prayschitta* (penances and expiation). The rites make a person pure, the dealings keep one's interactions pure, and penances purify people of the dirt that might have accumulated unknowingly over one's life.

One very important outlook of dharma developed in these works is the acceptance of a lower kind of dharma in which it is prescribed to act in one way, and a higher kind of dharma where staying away from that very act is considered more meritorious. For example, telling the truth is considered meritorious, but not telling the truth (when it is unpleasant) is considered to be more meritorious. Similarly, preaching dharma is meritorious, but not preaching dharma (when it harms or injures others) is considered to be more meritorious.

Thus, Smritis treat life as precious, and purity of purpose in life as more precious.

MANUSMRITI

Manusmriti is the oldest and the most authoritative work amongst Smritis, and has shaped the Hindu society much more deeply than it is realised. Most habits, practices, ethics, morality, etc. of a Hindu have descended directly from this book that has around 2700 shlokas, arranged in twelve chapters dealing with *achara, vyavahara,* and *prayaschitta*.

It is difficult to say when exactly this work was composed, but scholars believe that it got its final shape around second BCE. Mention of this book in *Mahabharata* on many occasions show that this work, even if not in the present form, was current in India well before Buddha walked on this earth. This book is so inclusive in nature that practically every later Smriti is based on this work.

The laws of succession, empowerment of women, the penal codes, and many other legal aspects practised in India are linked to the principles laid down in this book.

Content

Manu's work begins with the exposition of the universal concept of Hindu philosophy that God alone exists. The creation begins due to mysterious reasons, but it is an act of God. The soul, which in essence is inseparable from God, identifies itself with matter and runs after it through its senses that it gets with the body in which it is residing then. In the process, it acquires tendencies, and also gains virtues and vices, which in turn produce future tendencies. This vicious cycle of ignorance—desires—action—ignorance entangles a soul more and more in the trappings of the world. To come out of this cycle, one has to acquire the knowledge of the supreme God. This requires purity of mind, which can be attained only through a thorough cleansing of the body, mind and social conduct, and to preserve this purity, one must steer clear of every kind of further contamination. The more one is pure, the more important he is for the society, and is advanced towards spiritual realisation.

Dharma: The Path of Perfection

The guidelines of keeping oneself pure comes through dharma. According to Manu, dharma is to be known through the Vedas, Smritis, conduct of saints, and finally through one's own purified intellect. By following dharma, one attains perfection. Manu goes into detail on the duties of a student, householder, hermit, monk, and king, etc. He also discusses the principles of political administration and the vows and observances to be followed as expiation for the commission of certain sins. From there he goes on to discuss spiritual matters, safety, personal habits, cleanliness, sanitation, ways of conduct, and subjects of common sense.

The great lawgiver accepts that there is hardly any activity that is not prompted by desire (*kama*), but to act solely on such urges is *tamasik* (demeaning). It is to curb these base tendencies that dharma was promulgated by the sages. Manu stresses the importance of dharma by saying that one is born alone, one dies alone, and one enjoys the fruits of one's deeds alone. Father, mother, wife, children, and friends will not come to one's help in the other world; only dharma will rescue him. He finally sums up his instructions on dharma by saying that of all dharma, attainment of knowledge of self is supreme, since that is the only way to attain liberation from the cycles of birth and death.

Equality Through Sacrifice

The work of Manu is more than 2500 years old, and yet it approaches such levels of rationality and justice that one is left wonderstruck. His approach towards various issues has one fundamental rule— quality through sacrifice. Manu gives tremendous freedom and licenses to the educated and the cultured, but he also demands huge sacrifices from them, since quality can never come unless a person has sacrificed. While giving privileges to the Brahmins, he repeatedly asserts that a Brahmin who is not devoted to the Vedas and austerities, is not to be treated as a Brahmin, but as a Shudra. Such a fallen Brahmin's privileges, etc. are to be at par with a Shudra only.

Manu accepts the existence of customs peculiar to place, class, and families. He advises the conquering king to safeguard and maintain the customs of the conquered people, and yet consolidate his own empire. Today's India, despite all its diversity, is a culturally integrated country only because the Hindu kings of the past followed the political principles of Manu.

The Underprivileged in Manusmriti

Every religion has to spell out terms for its women and its masses. How a society treats its females, and how it treats the underprivileged, shows the level of culture and maturity acquired by it. In the context of the Smritis, the masses were the Shudras.

In the time of Manu and earlier, Shudras were those who were yet to imbibe the high standards of culture. They had not yet given up their basic tendencies of enjoyment and staying unclean—two important virtues of an upper caste. These two vices resulted in other personality faults like cruelty, selfishness, etc. All this meant that they had not yet become fit to climb the social hierarchy. Hence, they were given all kinds of licenses in matters of enjoyment (including meat eating, wine drinking, divorcing, etc.), but were prohibited from getting a lot of advantages, including the study of the Vedas.

Here it may be mentioned that to the sages, the knowledge of the Vedas was something like a copyrighted thing, and so, the choice of teaching a student was with the teacher. In general, the Shudras were not allowed to be taught the Vedas, but there were exceptions. Manu adds that a Shudra can attain the highest heaven exactly like a Brahmin simply by practising the good conduct of the Brahmins without studying the Vedas. The sage also instructs how a child of a Shudra woman can become a Brahmin over successive generations by marrying into the higher caste. Manu thus shows the way of upliftment of all through both external and internal means.

When it comes to women, Manu is both liberal and restrained regarding their powers and privileges. However, considering that this work is more than 2,000 years old, the liberty, rights, and the safety net that Manu creates for them is phenomenal. He writes, 'The husband, after conception by his wife, becomes an embryo and is born again of her; for that is the wifehood of a wife (*jaaya*) that the husband is born (*jaayate*) again by her. (9.6)… The gods dwell in homes where women are honoured; but where women are not honoured, no sacred rite yields rewards. (3.56)… One may give food, even before his guests, to the newly-married women, to infants, to the sick, and to pregnant women (3.114).'

He also believes that women have the power to sway the minds of men folk, irrespective of any existing relationship, 'Women do not care for beauty, nor is their attention fixed on age. They think it is enough that he is a man (9.14),' and they thus give themselves to the handsome and to the ugly, if they take a fancy to someone. So, women need to be treated with care and caution. He did not approve of giving license to women to move around wantonly, nor did he expect men to be harsh in dealing with women (9.4–13). 'Through their passion for men, through their mutable temper, through their natural heartlessness, they become disloyal towards their husbands, however carefully they may be guarded in this (world) (9.15).'

'No man can completely guard women by force; but they can be guarded by the practice of these: Let the husband employ his wife in the collection and expenditure of his wealth, in keeping everything clean, in the fulfilment of religious duties, in the preparation of his food, and in looking after the household utensils. Women, confined in the house under trustworthy and obedient servants, are not (well) guarded; but those who of their own accord keep guard over themselves, are well guarded. Drinking (hard liquor), associating with wicked people, separation from the husband, rambling abroad, sleeping (at unseasonable hours), and dwelling in other men's houses, are the six causes of the ruin of women. (9.10–13)'

On the other hand, Manu is particular about the rights and privileges of women, 'Reprehensible is the father who does not give his daughter in marriage at the proper time; reprehensible is the husband who does not keep his wife satisfied, and reprehensible is the son who does not protect his mother after her husband has died. (9.4)'

Special instructions are repeatedly given for the education of daughters, and the protection of sister, wife, and mother. He also introduced the concept of *stree dhan* (the property of a wife) which cannot be touched by the husband, 'But those male relatives who, in their folly, live on the separate property of women, e.g., appropriate the beasts of burden, carriages and clothes of women, commit sin and will sink into hell' (3.52). Her personal property goes to her children instead of going to her husband. Still another section makes it the duty of the king to protect the inherited and other property 'of wives and widows' against all aggressors. 'A righteous king must punish like thieves those relatives who appropriate the property of such females during their lifetime. (8.27–29)'

This kind of special protection in which relatives and the king is asked to take care of women, and then also adds the curse of God on those who cheat women's property, is unusual for any law book even in the present times anywhere in the world.

The ideas of marriage, remarriage, and adoption are extremely liberal in *Manusmriti*. Widow marriage and second marriage of females find clear mention here.

Import of Values

Manusmriti being a scripture, its ethics and values are aimed at making a person spiritual, instead of turning them out to be merely moral.

He categorises wrong acts in three: mental, verbal, and physical. 'Coveting the property of others, thinking of lustful things, and holding on to false doctrines (i.e. other than the Vedas), are the three mental sins. Abusing others, telling lies, ridiculing others, and idle talks are the four kinds of wrong verbal action. Taking what is not his, injuring others (even plant and animals) without the sanction of the law, and cohabit with other's wife, are declared to be the three kinds of wrong committed by the body (12.5–8).' Good karma and bad karma are the result of a person's abstinence from these wrong acts.

Contentment, truth, and non-violence are treated as important values. But truth for truth sake is discouraged, 'Speak the truth, speak the pleasing, but do not speak unpleasant truth, nor do ever utter pleasant lies.'

Manu takes a liberal view of certain indulgences, 'There is no sin in eating meat, in (drinking) spirituous liquor, and in carnal intercourse, for that is the natural way of created beings, but abstention brings great rewards (5.56)'.

Regarding positive acts that helps a person evolve, he says, 'By reciting the Vedas daily, by staying pure (at mental, verbal and physical level), by practising austerities, and by doing no injury to created beings, one comes to know of one's former births. He who continues with these practices even after recollecting his former existences, gains spiritual emancipation (4.148–9).'

These quotes give an idea of how Manu looks comprehensively at life and beyond it.

Ideas of Penance and Justice

The journey of life makes one commit mistakes unknowingly and at times knowingly. The blemish, seen or unseen, that comes to a person through such acts need cleansing that can be done through penances in case of acts committed by mistake, and through punishment for wilful negligence or indulgence. 'A man who omits a prescribed act, or performs a blameable act, or cleaves to sensual enjoyments, must perform a penance. Sages prescribe a penance for a sin unintentionally committed, while some other sages say that penance can be performed even for intentional offences. A sin unintentionally committed is got over by the recitation of Vedic texts, but those committed intentionally require different means. (11.44–46)'

When it comes to justice, Manu does not accept the present day truism, 'all are equal before justice…uniform civil code', and such catchy phrases that sound great but are hollow in substance. Manu believes that people are at different levels of evolution, and hence they need to be treated differently. So, he prescribes different punishment for different types of persons. This approach has come for severe criticism by certain groups in India in present times. Here it should be remembered that Smritis give secondary importance to the society in comparison to the individual, and hence, instead of uniform civil code, or a general moral code, Manu particularises values, as also the idea of justice.

More importantly Manu treats punishment as a kind of penance by which a person can get over his guilt, mistake, mischief, and misconduct to move ahead in life. Manu also does not treat punishment for a crime as deterrent to others. It is unfortunate that in present times punishment is associated with suffering, and people who have suffered demand punishment for the offender out of vengeance on the principles of tribal justice of Hammurabi, 'an eye for an eye'. The idea that state has to punish a person as penance and purification seems to have gone forever. This is natural, since no state cares for the spiritual upliftment for a person.

When punishment is accepted with grace by the punished, it becomes penance for him that takes him to the next level of spiritual evolution.

While delivering justice, the judge has to be considerate, 'He should punish first by (gentle) admonition, afterwards by (harsh) reproof, thirdly by a fine, after that by corporal chastisement (VIII.129).' Even in matters of evidence, the judge has to be liberal, 'Women should give evidence for women, and virtuous Shudras for Shudras, and men of the lowest castes for the lowest (VIII.68).'

One thus finds how Manu was clearly ahead of his time through his compassionate approach born of inclusiveness. It is unfortunate that the Indian society of later times could not really build on the outlook of this great law giver whose like has not yet walked on this globe.

Relevance in Present Times

The fluid nature of Smritis resulted in a large number of law books. If all the laws from these books be collected, there would be millions of them—enough to asphyxiate any society. That exactly is what these law books did; instead of being the instruments of freedom, these became the cages of confinement. Today they stand irrelevant, confined to the forgotten shelves of history in spite of the great principles that these contained, and the encouragement that they offered, 'A person must not despise himself on account of former failures. He must continue seeking fortune till death overcomes him, without ever despairing over his failure.'

The centre of existence for a Hindu progressively were widened in these law books from being individual to family, tribe, jati and finally to varna. This meant that instead of having thousands of smaller groups, India had four broad groups in which a person was born, and to which he identified. Whether good or bad, this system helped India survive the onslaught of covert and overt invasions for more than a 1,000 years.

But the days of the old law books are over.

The Indian Constitution and the Penal Code has done away with the law books from the past; growth of technology has done away with the jati; and the multinationals companies have taken away the family system. The march of machine and computers in the human society has completely demolished the *varnashrama* dharma, while the four *purusartha* (aims in life) are passe. Smritis were based on the principles of these two, and hence there is no way that any of these law books can ever be back. What to say of those laws, Indians do not even feel inclined to follow the ideals and codes of conduct of their ancestors. This has eroded the value system.

Worse, Indians are losing the ideals to live by, and they do not wish to follow any value system. Obedience to dollar, and worship of beauty seem to be the only accepted norms. This is making the new breed of Indians rootless, without any ideal, uncivil, immoral, and cruel. It can only get worse. It is time for a new Smriti that will be based on the principles of the past law givers, but will have a scintillating approach of modern times. Since the instructions of the Smritis were suggestive in nature, new Smritis came up to suit the changed times at a regular basis in India. Now it is time for a new Smriti that would keep the spiritual principles intact, and yet take care of the freedom and aspirations of today's liberated society.

It is difficult to say what exactly that new Smriti would be like, but it has to be there to take the Hindu race to a new high.

Philosophy is the essence of every religion.

— *Swami Vivekananda*

PHILOSOPHIES

Hindu Darshan

The various schools of Indian philosophy are known as *darshan*, which literally means 'as seen (by the sages)'. It applies to the way of life that can be taken up by the followers of that philosophy. So, Indian philosophy is not like Western philosophy that treats knowledge as a mind game. Indian sages proposed ways of life strictly based on how they perceived life in accordance with the Vedas, and lived by it. This makes Indian philosophy radically different from the Western philosophy.

The teachings of the philosopher-sages were usually written down in the form of a sutra (aphorism) that consisted a string of words. These sutras were committed to memory by the students that made it easy for them to remember the whole of a particular philosophy easily. With time there was a need for commentaries that could explain the sutras correctly. But this created situation when different commentators took up opposing stand on a particular sutra. This resulted in various schools of same philosophy. What we know today of different philosophies, have come to us through these commentaries.

Speculation and word play is a strict no-no in Hindu philosophy. A philosophy to be acceptable in Hinduism has to be based on the Vedas, and has to be preached by a sage. As mentioned earlier, there are six such Vedic philosophies—Samkhya by Kapil, Yoga by Patanjali, Nyaya by Gautama, Vaiseshika by Kanada, Mimamsa by Jaimini, and Vedanta by Vyasa. Of these, Vedanta has three major and some minor schools of thoughts, and it has come to be the chief philosophy of the Hindus. Other than these Vedic philosophies, there is the Charvaka philosophy of the materialists, and some schools based on Shiva and Shakti.

Generally philosophy begins with a basic enquiry like 'Who am I?', or 'Where have I come from?', 'What is the purpose of my life?', which often ends up in weltanschauung, a personal worldview that includes one's individual philosophical convictions. For example, most religious people have faith in a God, who is believed to be somewhere high up in the heaven, and who is always striving to keep us happy; his words are the scriptures that need to be respected, even if one does not study them; and, one must not indulge in any sacrilegious act against him, etc.

Whatever such convictions might be treated as, these are neither religious, nor philosophical. The way a housewife cannot be called a chemical engineer simply because she tinkers with spices in the kitchen, people with simplistic ideas about religion can never be called religious. One needs proper training to perform even the daily acts of life, but when it comes to religion, people think that they know everything. The consequence of a lack of proper understanding of religion is often seen when one faces internal or external crisis. In such moments, people just crack up. Worse, many end up being fanatics and killers.

Religion requires that its followers have a proper understanding of its dynamics, of which the most important is philosophy. A philosophy of life invariably discusses the origin of life, its extension, and the ultimate destiny. In the process it also has to discuss the methods of arriving at correct knowledge. Thus every philosophy discusses worldview, and methods of knowledge.

A philosophy can be worked out through pure reasoning, as is usually done in the Western philosophy, or it can be based on some scripture, as is done in every religion. Keeping in line with this, the systems of Hindu philosophy (major ones) are those that are based on the Vedas. The goal of each of these philosophies is to attain maximum blessedness in life, which means to attain mukti, liberation, from the cycles of life and death.

This work discusses only the worldview of the major Indian philosophies. The discussion on the methods of knowledge of these philosophies is given a miss due to their being highly technical.

CHARVAKA

The origin of Charvaka philosophy, the materialists, is not known for certain. *Mahabharata* does mention Charvaka, who preached against the Vedic philosophy, and there is a belief of him preaching the philosophy of 'eat, drink, and be merry' to lead vicious minds towards their doom.

Some scholars believe that this philosophy is rooted in the few verses of the Vedas that seem to propose free thinking. Since there was no organised following for the Charvaka school of thought the way there was for Epicureans of Greek philosophy, it may be presumed that it was worked out by some intelligent sage to show the fallacies associated with materialistic thought.

Charvaka philosophy preaches that the present life is the only truth that there is, and that can be. The human body is born out of lust, and death is the end of everything. After all, who has ever seen the dead return? So, the only goal of life is to seek maximum pleasure, even if it has to be carried out through credit or by other means.

There is no God, soul, heaven, or hell, according to this philosophy. Creation is effected by matter acting on matter, which at times results in new forms of matter like mind and consciousness, the way, say, common salt is produced by sodium and chlorine, both of which are deadly poison.

There is no law of karma. Whatever happens is due to chance and coincidence. The Vedas were written by scheming Brahmins to live off the fat of the naive. Austerities and spiritual practices are the greatest folly that one can indulge in, since there is no life after death; it is like not cooking food for fear of beggars coming for alms!

The only method of knowledge is through one's five senses, which means that inferential knowledge of the world, and the Vedic wisdom about God are of no use for those who have realised that seeking pleasure is the only truth in life.

It is surprising how most people adhere to this outlook of life, even though they think that they are religious. To be religious means to strive for God by giving up the worldly life, even if that be in small measures. Only when a person comes to accept his inherent weaknesses that he can hope to move ahead on the spiritual path.

SAMKHYA

Samkhya school of thought, founded by sage Kapila, is the oldest organised philosophy of India. For this reason, Kapila is also known as the Father of Indian philosophy. The name of this philosophy means 'right knowledge', which it professes to preach through its elaborate categorisation of nature and consciousness. Due to its antiquity and profundity, it shaped the Hindu religion, philosophy, and spirituality deeply. Yoga and Vedanta, the two major spiritual paths, draw heavily from its principles.

Samkhya relies on the doctrine of causation, according to which every effect is inherent and hence already present in its cause. Thus, a pot is already there in clay; the external agents and effort help the latent pot emerge from the visible clay. So, there is nothing that can be truly called new, or creation.

The world, according to it, is the interplay of two eternally existing entities—Purusha (spirit, consciousness, soul), and prakriti (matter, energy). Of these, prakriti has the power to be active but does not have independent consciousness, while Purusha has consciousness, but does not have independent mobility. Purusha are infinite in number, who are established in their own blissful state of existence, while prakriti is a single heap-like entity comprising of three gunas (qualities)—*sattva* (noble and stable), *rajas* (active), *tamas* (inert and sloth).

At the beginning of creation, the three *gunas* of prakriti that had stayed in a balance state till then, got disturbed. This resulted in their interacting with and overpowering each other, which threw up infinite permutations that resulted in the birth of various elements of the universe. Each of the individualised products (evolute of prakriti) is known as *tattva*, which are 24 in number: mind, the ten organs, the five elements, the five *tanmatras* (from which the senses and elements are born), cosmic ego, cosmic mind, and the prakriti herself. All these manifestations of nature were caused by the evolution of nature, and hence no external agent was required to materialise it.

Why creation? It is difficult to answer this question in any philosophy. Samkhya believes that creation is the interplay of consciousness and matter. Why and how these two come together may not be known, but the goal of their coming together is to give the Purusha experience of prakriti (*bhoga*, lit. enjoyment) through thoughts, locations, reward, punishment, etc., and then lead the soul to mukti (*apvarga*, lit liberation).

Whenever these two cross path, their inherent quality are induced on each other. Prakriti then appears conscious and the soul appears to be active. Prakriti has no intelligence of its own. As long as the Purusha is present in it, it appears as intelligent, which in reality is borrowed intelligence the way a planet's light is actually the reflected light of the sun. Purusha is pure intelligence, but when it comes in contact with prakriti, it starts experiencing the universe through the mind, which actually belongs to prakriti. During perception of any kind, the senses carry the sensations to its mind, but it is the soul where all different perceptions converge, get unified, and one becomes aware of it.

So, by nature the soul alone is free, but people wrongly attribute freedom to the mind, and thus give rise to the false idea of the mind being intelligent. When the soul gets into the contact with prakriti, it is enamoured by prakriti's beauty, and wants to enjoy it with gusto, forgetting its own divine nature. In the process it loves, hates, enjoys, suffers, dies, and gets reborn. After experiencing the charms of prakriti for an indefinite length of time, a soul (not all) eventually gets satiated and wants to get out of the realm of prakriti.

In spite of prakriti showing off its charms to Purusha, it is not really like an enchantress, but is more like a mother that guides the soul through her treasure land to making it realise its true nature, majesty, and glory. But for that, the soul has to crave freedom, which is through sadhana (spiritual practices) of discriminating between what belongs to prakriti, and what is the nature of soul. A constant awareness to give up all that is material (and hence belonging to prakriti) ultimately leads to the dawn of knowledge in the soul, when it realises its true nature of majesty and blissful existence. It then also realises how there never was any bondage, nor there was any freedom, since these were not real and binding at any stage.

Samkhya generally does not accept the existence of God. Its core belief lies only in consciousness (Purusha) and matter (prakriti) as two independent entities (dualism) that are responsible for creation, sustenance, and dissolution. In the process, one enjoys the world and then slowly moves towards beyond enjoyment.

Samkhya is a great philosophy whose rationality and simplicity is incomparable. In the long run, its principles and practices were adopted by Vedanta, and consequently these became important aspects of the Hindu way of life. One important aspect of sadhana in Vedanta, *neti-neti* (to be discussed in a later section) is a direct product of the practice of discrimination taught in Samkhya philosophy. And, the worldview of Vedanta comes straight from Samkhya. So much so, during philosophical arguments and debates, Samkhya is respectfully called the chief opponent of Vedanta.

YOGA

Yoga (also known as raja yoga—the royal yoga) is the science of spirituality that does not thrive on assumptions, axioms, beliefs, or traditions. It begins with the analysis of the working of mind—a truth that can never be denied—and from there it shows how a mind can be trained to do wonders, and can even be reined in completely to gain the knowledge of the self. Derived from the root *yuj*, the word 'yoga' (pronounced yog, and not yoga) means union. The term is also used in a special sense by the practitioners of different paths of spiritual realisation—to a karma yogi it signifies the union between an individual and the whole; to a raja yogi (mystic) it means the union between his lower and the higher self; to a *bhakta* (devotee of God) it implies the union between himself and God; and to a *jnani* (*vedantin*) it stands for the non-duality of existence.

Yoga (or, raja yoga) is a fully developed philosophy with a well-defined worldview. At the same time, it is also a practical manual of spiritual practices in which the focus is on maximising the use of psycho-physical faculties of a person for the realisation of the highest truth. Yogis believe that by controlling one's body, and by focussing the mind, a practitioner can attain anything in life, including mukti. The most important of these manuals is Patanjali's Yoga Sutras. Yoga was current in India for a long time, and it is believed that Patanjali compiled the Yoga Sutras around 2nd/3rd century BCE. However, like all other Hindu sacred texts, the controversy rages as to its exact date.

Since yoga deals with the mind, it is also known as Hindu psychology. But unlike the present day psychology, the discussion in yoga is more thorough, meaningful, and with a higher purpose. The analysis and remedy of spiritual issues presented here are non-sectarian in nature. This makes yoga universally relevant and useful.

One branch of yoga is called hatha yoga, in which emphasis is laid upon postures, purification of the body and nerves, and breath control. This kind of practise leads to a healthy body and long life, but does not lead to liberation. Due to this reason, many refuse to accept Hath yoga (the popular yoga) as a valid branch of philosophy.

The philosophy of yoga is based entirely on the Samkhya philosophy, as discussed above. Thus yoga accepts the concept of Purusha (soul) and prakriti (matter). Yoga makes only a passing reference to life after death. Concepts like God, heaven, hell, sin, etc. do not get much importance in it, although law of karma and the consequent baggage produced by it in an individual, gets importance. The goal is to burn down the storehouse of karma through self-knowledge, without which one would continue to be born again and again.

The lack of theological ideas in its philosophy gives yoga a practical approach, making it the philosophy of belonging to here and now, with the precision and clarity of a demonstrable experiment in a laboratory.

It is well known how the mind gets inputs from the external and the inner world that makes it throw reactions towards that impulse. This reaction is commonly known as 'knowledge'. Yoga is about restraining the mind from throwing those reactions. It is through this restraining, with the help of meditative techniques that one slowly learns to disassociate from everything around him.

The state of restraining the mind completely from taking in any impulse is known as samadhi. In that state (the highest state of meditation), one becomes completely free from every kind of association and gets liberated from the cycle of birth and death.

As is evident, people have different kinds of mind. Yoga categorises these into five. The first one is the hyperactive type whose activities lead one to pleasure and pain. The second one is dull types that tends to injure others. These are the ordinary minds. The third type of mind is of those who are consciously struggling to concentrate. The fourth type is of those whose concentration has gone deeper. In this state the mind gains the capability to concentrate on one object for a long time. The fifth type is the one-pointed form in which the mind succeeds in concentrating fully that results in Samadhi. These five types of minds are also known as mental stages, since one type can change into another through regular practices of yoga.

Whatever the type of mind, it stays in a particular state characterised by thoughts that are the reaction of the mind to the external or inner impulses. This state of mind's reaction (thought) is called *vritti*. There is never a condition when the mind is not occupied with some *vritti*, which are also of five kinds—knowledge (through senses, reasoning, or scriptures), illusions (mistaking a rope for a snake), word-play with no related reality (oxymoron, as when says 'cold fire'), dreams, and memories. The goal for a yogi is to get out of all these five kinds of mental states (mentioned in the previous para), and stop the *vritti*s associated with them (Yoga Sutra, 1.2). This requires great practice and perseverance for a long time. The Yoga Sutras discuss the ways, means and the result of the conscious control of the mind.

According to yoga, knowledge (*vritti*) comes in the package of three: *Shabda* (impulse from the senses), *artha* (corresponding meaning of it), and jnana (knowledge of that impulse). When the brain receives the signal and processes it for the use of mind; the process is known as *artha*. When the mind grasps the meaning of the shabda, it throws out its individualised reaction towards the object from which the signal came. This individualised reaction to the external impulse is known as jnana. These three are distinct processes, but get mixed up in such a fashion as to stay indistinct to a common man. One perceives only their combined effect, known as external object. But, a yogi who has attained a level of meditation can distinguish the three, and if he wants he can acquire miraculous powers by the application of this power of his mind. Mukti too comes only through the disassociation of these three, and by focussing only on jnana.

Yoga prescribe eight 'limbs' or steps prescribed to self-realisation: *yama* (control of basic impulses) *niyama* (practise of virtues), *asana* (sitting with firmness), *pranayama* (control of breath), *pratyahara* (withdrawing the senses from their respective objects and then keeping them held back), *dharana* (contemplation), *dhyana* (meditation) and *samadhi*.

As one practises these, the growth of a yogi comes in stages—the restlessness of the mind to know a thousand things of the world stops, the mind goes beyond feeling pain at anything of the universe, the sense of duty towards anything in the world drops away, the mind becomes completely free of any kind of agitation, complete control over mind comes, and finally one gets established in one's self.

Yoga teaches that since all power of the universe flows from the mind, be it individual, or universal, a yoga practitioner can gain powers simply by practising the related disciplines. It may be noted here that these powers have actually been seen manifested in great yogis.

As one progresses in the attainment of concentration, a time comes when the mind becomes completely focussed on itself, stopping it from taking any external or inner impulse. It is then that one realises that he is beyond and superior to prakriti; that he depends on nothing in the universe, and desires nothing. It is then that the soul attains *kaivalya* (lit. uniqueness, freedom and perfection). He then also realises that he was never born, nor did he ever die, but these were mere sights offered by the nature. He realises that, as a soul, he was never moving, but it was the nature that was moving all along that was getting reflected on it, making it believe that it was moving, enjoying and suffering. This is mukti.

Samkhya does not pay importance to God, but yoga accepts God (Isvara) as one who is the special soul (Purusha), untouched by misery, actions, their results, and desires, but He is not described as the creator of the universe, since creation depends on Purusha and prakriti. Isvara is infinite since his knowledge is unlimited, and hence he is the teacher of teachers. The worldly teachers are all limited, but he is the teacher of infinite knowledge; his manifesting word is Aum; one can attain samadhi by repeating the sacred Aum, and by thinking on its meaning. One may also get the same results by meditating on God.

It can thus be seen how yoga develops the sadhana mode of Samkhya philosophy, and makes it practicable. Later, Vedanta took its ideas about mind, and meditation techniques to help people rise higher on the ladders of spirituality.

NYAYA

The great sage Gautama, also known as Akshapada, is credited with the Nyaya school of thought that thrives on Vedic wisdom, along with a well-defined rationalism and logic. Nyaya means 'that which is right', and is applied to this philosophy since it concerns with correct thinking, and also with the means to acquiring the true knowledge of reality. The importance of logic in the system has earned it the name 'logical realism'.

The aim of Nyaya is liberation of the individual soul, as it is with every other Indian philosophy, through a thrust on clear thinking born of proper reasoning. The arguments and logic used in Nyaya, chiselled over thousands of years, are so subtle and intricate that only great scholars trained in the system can truly understand and make use of them. This makes Nyaya out of bounds for a common man, but its methodology of reasoning made Hinduism such a strong religion that no theology could ever uproot it. Later, Shankaracharya built his arguments for Vedanta on the lines of Nyaya logic that made it a complete system of thought, with extreme subtlety and yet great profundity.

The elaborate discussion in Nyaya on logic to bring out the meaning of a statement correctly is central to this philosophy. However, it is neither necessary nor possible to discuss those intricacies. Here the discussion is only on the salient features of Nyaya's views related to religion.

Nyaya accepts the self (soul) as a unique substance (note the term 'substance') that experiences feelings like desire, pain, pleasure, etc. There are different selves in different bodies, and hence the experience of one does not overlap with the other. The self is indestructible, eternal, and infinite, since it is not limited by time and space, even though it is a substance. Consciousness is not an inherent trait of the self, but it arises due to its identification with mind and senses. To be liberated means to disjoin the self from its identification with the mind. This results in permanent cessation of pain, and attainment of eternal bliss.

The deliverance, mukti, does not come easily to a self. One has to first study the Vedas, then understand the import of the statements therein by reasoning them out, and finally by meditating on the meaning of those statements. Thus, if someone wants to have illumination through Gayatri mantra, he has to first know about it, understand its meaning in depth, and then meditate on the meaning.

In spite of one's spiritual efforts, one requires the grace of God to attain knowledge that liberates a person. In fact, nothing happens in the world without his grace. Here it is interesting to note how the most logical system of the Indian thought stresses on the importance of the grace of God.

God is the eternal, infinite self who creates, maintains, and destroys the universe. The creation is not out of nothing, but it is carried out of the eternally existing atoms, space, time, ether, minds, and souls. These six eternal substances are coexistent with God who puts them into order to create the non-eternal universe. God is also the moral governor of the universe who, like a loving father, directs all souls to good and bad, and then gives the fruits of those acts. The acts of a soul (in any of the spheres of existence) are strictly according to the will of God who keeps the self either under bondage of the non-eternal world, or liberates it to its true nature of being eternal.

Nyaya gives ten proofs of the existence of God. The arguments used therein are so extensive that these cover the entire range of arguments for the existence of God as used in the Western religious philosophy.

The pluralistic realism of there being God and six more realities (Samkhya has only two realities, and Vedanta has only one) that Nyaya offers as the spiritual truth, is unfortunately not as satisfying as its logic. Indeed, the real worth of Nyaya lies in its theory of knowledge that is unparalleled even from the Western standards. But unlike the Western logic, the logical realism of Nyaya is not a mere intellectual gymnastic, but is applied to address issues related to life, existence, and reality that throws up conclusions which have permeated deep in the Hindu religious life.

Later, Vedanta delved deep in the logical system of Nyaya to come up with a complete system that was logical to the hilt, and was also spiritually sound. There are, of course, a good number of

Nyaya scholars who go strictly by its system, while condemning Vedanta through their rigorous reasoning skills that have been honed over thousands of years.

VAISESHIKA

Vaiseshika school of thought was founded by the great sage Kanada (pronounced Kanaad), who was a great ascetic of his time. This philosophy is seen and studied conjointly with Nyaya due to a large number of similarities between them. They both accept liberation of the individual soul as the goal of life; ignorance as the root cause of misery; reality of the universe; and, categorisation of objects (lit. *padartha*) that cause creation.

This philosophy is mostly an elaboration and a close study of *padartha* (objects), the right knowledge of which is considered essential to the correct understanding of the universe that helps one get out of ignorance, and be free. *Padartha* is anything that can be denoted by a word, and hence is real. These *padartha* can be categorised into seven—substance (*dravya*), quality (*guna*), action (*karma*), generality (*samanya*), particularity (*visesha*), relation (*samavaya*), and non-existence (*abhava*). Of these, the first six stand for all that exist, and the last one is for all that does not exist. The philosophy derives its name from *visesha* (particularity) that it discusses in good measure, along with the other objects. Of course, it is beyond the scope of this paper to discuss these.

Of the seven *padarthas* elaborated in Vaiseshika, the most interesting one is *abhava* (non-existence), which is treated as a positive entity, as is commonly used in statements like, 'he was conspicuous by his absence'. *Abhava* as a *padartha* plays an important role in Vaiseshika philosophy, and later, it was taken up by Vedanta that helped it build a strong foundation for itself.

Vaiseshika treats the world composed of the seven *padarthas* (instead of 16 *padarthas* of Nyaya philosophy), as the great gymnasium where the individual soul acquires knowledge and consequently liberation. The physical universe is accepted to be created by four types of atoms—earth, fire, water, and air that have related properties as perceived by different sense organs. These atoms (*anu*) are eternal and exist independent of each other. At the time of creation, these start interacting with each other, resulting in formation of the dyad (two atoms), also known as *parmanu* (molecules). When three dyads combine, it is called triad. This is the minimum perceptible object by the senses. The universe is composed of the four kinds of atoms in the form of the single atoms, dyads, triads, and the larger compounds born of these.

This concept of atoms as the foundation of the universe, earned the name 'atomists' for Vaiseshika. But this atomism is different from that of Greek philosophy, as also from modern physics. In these Western concepts, atoms are free, and combine randomly to create the universe and its objects through a blind chance. It is not so in Vaiseshika, which treats the universe and its constituents to belong to a moral order governed by God. There is no blind chance, nor is there any scope for unlicensed acts anywhere in the universe.

The creation itself takes place when God (Maheshwara) wills so, but the creation is beginningless in time, and hence there is never a first creation, nor it is one-off affair. Creation means destruction of the order that existed prior to it, and hence there is always a stock of good and bad associated with it. This stock is known as *adrishta* (lit. unknown), and it plays an important role in shaping the destiny of everyone.

God is the creator and destroyer of the universe, but he is transcendent and separate from the world. So, he does not interfere in the affairs of the world that runs strictly on the laws of karma.

Every living being is in reality the soul that experiences good or bad according to its acts and understanding. The results of acts come to a person not only from the physical laws governing the universe (e.g. fire burns if one puts one's hand in it), but also from the universal moral law of karma. The goal of each soul is to get out of the bondages created by the *padarthas* that creates pain and misery in one's minds and be free.

These four orthodox philosophies, discussed above, accepted the Vedas as supreme in spiritual matters, although these were not based strictly on the Vedas; there were logical thinking, as also intuitive wisdom of the sages. The truly committed Vedic schools of philosophy are two: Mimamsa and Vedanta.

MIMAMSA

Mimamsa means 'the solution arrived after critical thinking and investigation'. This school of philosophy, founded by the sage Jaimini, discusses dharma—the right way of life. According to Mimamsa philosophy, the goal of life is to live by dharma as detailed in the Vedas. So, to know dharma, and act accordingly, one has to have a correct methodology of interpretation of the Vedic texts, and also the philosophical justification of the rituals detailed in the Vedas to find out the right dharma.

The word 'ritual' brings to mind the semi-literate priests who are usually seen in a recital or a ritualistic mode. But Mimamsa had the best Indian minds of the period as its adherents, and it was the most popular philosophy in India till it was overtaken by Vedanta.

When Shankaracharya waded through Indian philosophical minds to take Hinduism across them forever, his most powerful opponents in matters of reasoning were the Mimamsa philosophers like Kumarila Bhatt and Mandan Mishra.

Mimamsa developed elaborate mechanism to discuss the nature of knowledge, as also the nature and criterion of truth and falsity. Epistemology, the method of knowledge, is discussed so soundly in this system that Vedanta drew heavily from it to build its own method of knowledge. It accepts six methods of knowledge—sense knowledge, reasoning, comparison, scriptures, postulations, and non-perception. It is not possible to discuss these in detail here, but suffice it to say that the methods of knowledge play an important role in every philosophy, both Indian and Western. How these are defined and accepted, make a system stay or collapse in the long run.

Mimamsa accepts the world as real and eternal, meaning that it neither gets created nor destroyed. The souls are eternal and permanent spiritual substances that inhabit the many worlds (like heaven, etc.). The eternal worlds and the eternal souls are governed by the law of karma, which is considered sufficient to explain the formation of objects and bodies in the universe. When a soul has experienced the results of his past action that can be got through that particular body, it gives up that body and moves over to a new world to acquire a new body to work out the unfinished karma, and also gather new ones. This has been continuing, and will continue till eternity. Gita talks of this philosophy of eternal births and deaths based on this philosophy in the famous verse, 'one who is born, dies; and one who dies, is born again' (Gita,II.27).

Most surprisingly, Mimamsa does not accept the existence of God! Surprising because, this was the most popular philosophy in the Indian households. It does accept the existence of gods like Indra and others, but it does not accept the idea of one God who rules the universe. The followers of this school respect the Vedas so much that they do not accept that there can be anything superior to the Vedas, which are the self-existent knowledge. The Vedas are the final authority in matters of righteousness, and the mantras are capable of producing any result that one may wish for. There are innumerable stories in *Mahabharata* and *Ramayana* where people are seen to have their objective fulfilled through yajna, which is a form of karma (action). The Brahmins boasted that they could even control gods by the power of the yajna and the mantras!

Karma is explained through two important concepts of *shakti* and *apurva* (the unseen). *Shakti* is the potential energy, as in seed, that gets expressed if it does not meet with obstruction or destruction. The second one, *apurva*, is the soul's potency to enjoy what it has done in the past. So, if someone performs a yajna to go to heaven, then the soul acquires the unperceived potency, *apurva*, that bears fruit when the time is appropriate.

The highest good, according to Mimamsa, is to attain the highest heaven where there is unalloyed bliss. However, the followers of Mimamsa realised with time that even such heavens cannot be eternal. So, they slowly started talking of liberation as the highest goal, although there is no unanimity about the experiences of the soul in that state.

It is normal to wonder if these philosophies have any relevance in the present age that values utility more than idle thinking. Well, the answer is both yes and no. For a materialist, as also for those who have chosen a spiritual path and are travelling on it with commitment, there is no need of these philosophies. But all those who are still green on the path of religion, particularly, Hinduism, have to pass through stages when their mind gets coloured by the principles of one or more of these philosophies. At heart everyone is a logician, believer, analyst, etc., and hence a time may come when one may look at religion through that format. At such moments these philosophies, and also the arguments used to counter them prove useful and effective.

The five philosophies—Samkhya, Yoga, Nyaya, Vaiseshika, and Mimamsa—although not a common man's cup of tea, played a crucial role in shaping the worldview of the Indians. More than that, each of these five contributed mightily in fine tuning the Vedanta philosophy that has come to be the main philosophy of the Indian race.

VEDANTA

It was mentioned in the Upanishad section that there are three outlooks to them. These three outlooks, Dvaita, Visishtadvaita, and Advaita, are now collectively known as Vedanta. These three philosophies encompass not only whole of Hinduism, but the entire world of religions. Highlighting this fact, Swami Vivekananda said,

> [T]his is the essential of religion: the Vedanta, applied to the various ethnic customs and creeds of India, is Hinduism. The first stage, i.e. Dvaita, applied to the ideas of the ethnic groups of Europe, is Christianity; as applied to the Semitic groups, Mohammedanism. The Advaita, as applied in its yoga-perception form, is Buddhism, etc. Now by religion is meant the Vedanta; the applications must vary according to the different needs, surroundings, and other circumstances of different nations.

Vedanta has come to be seen as the ultimate philosophy of the Hindus in the present times. Every Hindu practices it in some form either knowingly or unknowingly. By its very character Vedanta is all encompassing and hence a hugely tolerant philosophy that gives it a massive catholicity and makes it a favourite of the masses. The general character of the Hindu religion—commitment to God, and universal acceptance—are the traits of Vedanta too, which makes it seem probable that a time may come when Hinduism and Vedanta would be synonymous.

Unlike every other philosophy of the world, Vedanta has no founder. In that sense too, it is similar to Hinduism, which is as eternal as a religion can be. The word Vedanta literally means the 'end of the Vedas', which may imply the Upanishads, or may mean the 'purpose of the Vedas'. In either case, it means the philosophy that emerges from the Vedas and the Upanishads.

Seen philosophically, Vedanta is based on the principles of spirituality as recorded in the Upanishads and the Gita. Later, Vyasa is believed to have written Brahma Sutra, which is a treatise on Vedanta in sutra form (aphorisms). These three works—Upanishads, Gita, and Brahma Sutras—are treated as the foundation books of Vedanta. Later sages wrote commentaries on these three books to bring out their import as they understood it. This gave rise to different schools of Vedanta.

Of these different schools, three major ones are Advaita (non-dual) popularised by Shankaracharya, Visishtadvaita (qualified non-dualism) popularised by Ramanuja, and Dvaita (dualism) popularised by Madhvacharya.

These three schools of Vedanta have been current in India since ancient times, but the three teachers gave them their philosophical base, and also popularised them. Other than these three, there are hundreds of other schools, but they are not as popular.

Of the many schools of Vedanta, Advaita is considered to be philosophically sound, while Visishtadvaita and Dvaita are more popular. Dvaita and Visishtadvaita are known as Bhakti schools of Vedanta, since these do not accept the non-duality of the individual with the universal, as Advaita Vedanta does. They both accept Isvara (God) as the supreme creator, having qualities, and accept the soul as inferior to him. Visishtadvaita shows how the soul is related to God the way a leaf is related to a tree, while Dvaita shows how soul is related to God as a servant is related to the Master.

The goal of Vedanta, as of every other Indian philosophy (not the Charvaka), is mukti—liberation. Vedanta does this by discussing the nature of relationship between the self (*jiva*) and God (Brahman). The difference in the perception of this relationship results in different schools of Vedanta that was mentioned earlier. These differences also erupt due to their emphasis on certain statements of the source books, along with their reasoning skills, and use of grammar to prove what they want to prove. Here it may be mentioned that Sanskrit language uses many words for the same object, and the same word is used to denote many objects. This quirk is of great advantage in poetry and logic, but it is disastrous when it comes to bringing out the meaning of a sentence. Due to this, it is nearly impossible to understand the scriptures without a proper commentator, which is invariably coloured by the understanding of the commentator.

The idea of God in Vedanta (all the schools) is strictly based on what the Upanishads say about him. Vedanta only makes the meaning of the Upanishad statements clear and coherent. It was mentioned in the chapter on Upanishads how the sages have described Brahman both as formless, and also as with form who has qualities like knowledge, power, strength, glory, compassion, etc.

Seen from the standpoint of spiritual experiences, a mind that has been made pure through sadhana comes to perceive God as having form and qualities. This aspect of God is known as Isvara.

But there is also a state when a mind becomes so completely absorbed in God that the duality of the perceiver and the perceived vanishes. In that state what remains, cannot be expressed in words. This state of reality is called Brahman, which is beyond all qualities and all descriptions. The self (atman) is then realised to be one with Brahman (not with Isvara).

These three schools of Vedanta, along with some others, seem to confuse the first-time readers of Vedanta philosophy. But the important thing to note about them is that Shankaracharya's Vedanta accepts the other schools as equally valid till one accepts the existence of mind even in the final stages of realisation. This fact was later corroborated by Sri Ramakrishna too, which means that the three outlooks—Advaita, Visishtadvaita, and Dvaita—are the three facets of the same reality. Both Shankaracharya and Sri Ramakrishna present the complete picture of Vedanta, while everyone else, even those who profess to be Advaita follower, present only the part picture.

Going through these philosophies, one may wonder as to why there are so many different opinions emerging out of the same scriptures? The main reason behind these differences is largely because the sages based their philosophies in line with the Vedas, which are not a systematically written book, but are mere collection of spiritual realisations of different sages. A lack of systematised presentation invariably results in varied opinion in any field. What to say then of the world of religion that presupposes a particular mindset! Another reason behind the differences is the limits of logic and language in explaining how the infinite (God) creates the finite (world).

In spite of all the differences, every Hindu philosophy agrees on certain points like importance of scriptures to know about spiritual matters, atman as the true reality behind a person, transmigration of soul, and, mukti as the goal of life. These traits, when accepted in full, make one a Hindu.

Advaita Vedanta

It was Shankaracharya who gave Vedanta an unshakeable philosophical base, and also helped to popularise it all over the country.

Shankaracharya was born in c. 788 CE in Kaladi, Kerala. Since his childhood, he proved to be a remarkable child with divine abilities. The tradition has that he left his home and his weeping widow mother to become a monk when he was just eight years old. Wandering in search of his guru, he reached Omkareshwar where he became a disciple of Govindapada from whom he learnt Vedanta, and then got down to writing his treatise on them and spreading the message of Vedanta throughout the country. In the process, he defeated all the major philosophers of the land. He was only 16 then. For the next 16 years he continued with his marvellous work, and he gave up his body when he was just 32.

Shankaracharya's philosophy came to be known as Advaita Vedanta since he talked about the ultimate reality as non-dual. But he was not sectarian, as he came to be portrayed in later times. His approach was completely inclusive, just like the approach of Vyasa, and that of Sri Ramakrishna in the 20th century. His philosophy is not like a marauding army that annihilates its enemy, it is rather like an ocean that embraces every river in its bosom and gives them a new greater identity. For example, he accepts the idea of creation as in Samkhya, meditation techniques as in Yoga, logical skills of Nyaya–Vaiseshika, and stresses the importance of religious activity (or activities done religiously) as in Mimamsa. On the religious front too, he harmonised the practices of every sect prevalent in the period, and in recent times it has come to accept every religion as a path to realisation, as practised and preached by Sri Ramakrishna. Thus Advaita Vedanta does not leave out anything; it just assigns a place to everything in the grand scheme of God, all the while stressing the fact that God alone exists.

The arguments used by Shankaracharya are so powerful that no other philosophy or religion could ever gain eminence in India. His central argument is that one holds oneself as dear, although the idea of self may be different with different people. The crude minds treat their body, their children, and property as dear, while the evolved ones treat their mind, and the indwelling self as dear. He goes one step further to show that atman, the reality within, is the true self of all, and hence it is the real thing to be coveted in life. Whatever joy one experiences in the world, is because one sees one's own self in that. In the final state of self-realisation, one knows that he is non-different from Brahman, the supreme reality behind the universe. The highest good of a person lies in attaining this knowledge.

The supreme reality is Brahman (meaning the great), who is both the creator and the material for the creation. This means that there is no duality of any kind in the universe—whatever is there, is Brahman, *sarvam khalu idam Brahma*. But, Brahman cannot be said to be one, since the idea of one presupposes duality. So, Advaita Vedanta does not talk of reality as one (monism), but as non-dual (beyond the idea of single or multiplicity). This should not make one think that it is zero (*shunya* of Buddhism), since the idea of existence persists even when everything else becomes non-existent. Some of these arguments have been mentioned in passing in the sections on the Upanishads and Gita.

Creation, according to Advaita Vedanta, is effected through maya (i.e. not directly by God), which is the divine power of God, and is indistinguishable from him. Maya is similar to prakrti of Samkhya, but maya does not have the independence of prakrti. This means that any creation is only an apparent change, the way a gold ornament is in reality gold only. Another example used in Vedanta is that of the ocean and waves. A wave is apparently different from another wave, and is definitely not the ocean. But once a wave subsides, its limited reality merges with the universality of ocean. The wave then realises that it was all along the ocean. Its transformation as a wave was not real, but apparent. This apparent transformation of the real into the unreal is called maya.

Like every other Indian philosophy, Advaita accepts that knowledge about God cannot be arrived at through senses, since God is not an object. Nor can his existence be proved logically, since a sharper mind will disprove the proved. The only way to know about God, mukti, rebirth, heaven, etc. is through scriptures. The validity of the scriptures should not be questioned since these are the records of the intuitive wisdom of sages who had purified their minds through intense sadhana, and they did not have any selfish motive.

Shankaracharya does not go only by the words of scriptures, but stresses that the knowledge of reality must pass through the tests of *shruti* (Vedas), *yukti* (reasoning), and *anubhuti* (personal experience). Thus, a person may claim himself to be an incarnation of God or a prophet, but for this fact to be accepted, it has to pass through the three parameters of truth. It also means that unless a person realises God, his words about God do not have any validity.

This paper is meant only to give an idea of what Advaita Vedanta is, and hence it is beyond its scope to give an inkling of the depth of reasoning used by Shankaracharya. The logical skill and dialectical subtlety used by him, and later by his learned followers, attain heights where the intellectual lungs of the ordinary would explode. In recent times, personalities like Swami Vivekananda and Ramana Maharshi have given a further boost to Advaita Vedanta.

Visishtadvaita

Shankaracharya does not go unchallenged. Ramaunja (11th CE), and then Madhvacharya (13th CE) challenged some of the ideas of Shankaracharya to establish the other two famous schools of Vedanta, known as Visishtadvaita, and Dvaita respectively. Ramanuja not only challenged Shankara's standpoint but also, apparently, defeated it and established the system in which devotion and rituals get more importance than reasoning of Advaita Vedanta. Thus if Shankaracharya's outlook is based on reasoning, Ramanuja touches the emotions. This gave an immense sense of self-respect to the minds of the common man, who had been feeling left out in the race of philosophical religion. Since then, Indian thinkers and spiritual seekers have taken sides with these two great minds of India. However, despite the intellectual correctness of Shankara, it is Ramanuja's words that appeal the heart of a common seeker, and when put on the balance of rationality and practicality, Ramanuja's approach comes out the winner.

Ramanuja was born in Sriperumbudur, near Chennai in Tamil Nadu in 1017 CE, and is believd to have lived for 120 years. He was married but he gave up all for the sake of spirituality that brought him from one teacher to another till he met Yamunacharya from whom he learnt the philosophy of qualified non-dualism. Then onwards he got down to preaching *Sharanagati* (surrender) to God as the means to *moksha*. In the process, this philosophy accepts that the world is created by God from matter (prakriti) that exists in him. Creation is a real act of God, and not a mere play of name and form as Advaita Vedanta believes. Maya, the power of God, is as wonderful as God himself. To him, maya stands for God's power of creating wonderful objects. So, it is not false as Advaitins believe. Creation and the created world are not illusory.

God of Ramanuja is the Brahman of Vedanta who is in fact Narayana. He is a being who has truth, knowledge, omniscience, compassion, etc. as qualities, and not as essence. This is a major departure from Advaita that considers these qualities as the nature of God, and not as his qualities. God is the creator, has the form which is the quintessence of beauty and attractiveness. He is the *antaryamin* (indweller) of all beings, and only he can grant mukti. God contains within himself the material objects and also the finite souls which are real, and not illusory as *advaitins* hold. Thus Visistadvaita means Advaita (because of the unity of Brahman), with qualities (*visista*, due to the possession of the conscious and the insentient, which are the real parts).

Ramanuja's philosophy is also known as Sri Vaishnavism, in which the concept of Sri (the divine consort of the Lord) has great importance. Due to this, God is also known as Sri Narayana. However, unlike in Tantra, Sri does not play any particular part in the creative function of the Lord. She is quite unlike Shakti, the female counterpart of Shiva. Vishnu himself is the great creator and Sri is always with him and ever established on his chest.

It is unthinkable, according to Ramanuja, that man who is finite can be identical with God in every respect. Man is not different from him in the sense that he pervades and controls man as well as every other thing in the universe. As the soul controls the body, so God controls the soul. The identity is in this sense. The human body and the soul are both finite. The soul is eternal but infinitely small (*anu*). Thus Ramanuja's idea of soul is exactly the opposite of Shankara's concept, in which the soul is infinite. Though small, the soul makes the whole body conscious, and also becomes identified with it.

Jivanmukti, an important concept in Advaita, does not find any favour with Ramanuja. According to him, karma (and not ignorance, as in Advaita) is the cause of bondage, and hence liberation is attained only when the body perishes.

Ramanuja's main interest was to link devotion with the Vedanta. To him the ecstatic devotion to the Lord was far important than philosophy. Every school of Bhakti in later times drew heavily from Ramanuja to uphold its standpoint.

Dvaita

And then came Madhvacharya (also known as Madhva), who was born in 1238 CE near Udupi, Karnataka. He was of a heavy built and a very sharp mind with prodigious memory and phenomenal scholarship. By the time he was 16, he became a monk, and devoted himself to spreading his philosophy, known as Dvaita Vedanta. His life was full of miracles and miraculous achievements related to his body, mind, and spiritual powers till he gave it up when he was 79. It is interesting to see how all the three great teachers of Vedanta came from South India.

The main tenet of Madhva's Dvaita Vedanta is that the Vedic tradition teaches a fundamental difference between the soul and Brahman. This is markedly different from Advaita Vedanta, which Madhva attacked with gusto. His philosophy belongs to the Realist school of Indian philosophy and is in the same category as

Samkhya, Nyaya, Vaisheshika, and Purva Mimamsa schools. They believe that the universe is a real creation of God. The plurality of souls are bound by a real bondage due to the primordial ignorance. But unlike others, Madhva coupled his realism with high devotion and the worship of Vishnu. This is why his philosophy continues to be as vibrant today as it was in his own time, while the other systems of realism are dead.

Madhva insists on a clear distinction between atman and Brahman. According to him, the former is unquestionably dependent upon, and also fundamentally different from the latter. This means that the Lord has a complete transcendence over the human soul. For Madhva, this view alone makes bhakti (devotion) an essential component of religious belief and practice. Attaining the Lord's grace is the soul's only hope of achieving moksha (liberation) from the cycle of rebirth.

The souls are eternal, and are not created by God as in the Semitic religions. The souls are dependent, but not generated by God, and co-exist with him eternally, supported by his will and entirely controlled by him. By following the concept that souls are not created by God and also classifying them, Madhva provides a lucid answer to the problem of evil. He seeks the solution to the riddle of evil in the intrinsic nature of the soul itself. Often, evil behaviour displayed in the world might not be just the nature of the soul but may also be dependent upon the timeless actions (karma) of the soul itself. This way Madhva got rid of a very serious theological problem that every dualistic religion has to face.

Madhva was motivated into presenting his philosophy in contradiction to the greats like Shankara and Ramanuja by his conviction that one must stay true to experience above everything. He never believed in pure consciousness that did not involve subject-object relationship. To him, even dreamless sleep was a kind of experience, and so was samadhi. He was committed to reasoning. Even his critics agree that he was perfect in presenting arguments. But, he made a free use of licenses offered by Sanskrit grammar, and he also used a system of finding meaning of the Vedic texts by the Mimamsaka system of philosophy. These gave him a great freedom, and based on these, his arguments are irrefutable. All his actions, words, and philosophy were driven by his fervent devotion to Lord Vishnu. It was his one desire to establish the supremacy of bhakti above everything else. Also, he had a strong desire to work out a philosophy that would not only explain the contradictions of the Upanishads, but also unify and harmonise the later scriptures like the Puranas. In short, Madhva believes that sadhana through Vishnu bhakti is the only way to be released from bondage.

The overview of the philosophies in this short section gives an idea of how the Hindus look at themselves and the world around them. The one thing that truly matters is the intense desire to be free from the bonds of the world. This is spirituality. This is the goal of Hindu religion and the Hindu race.

THE FUTURE

Living Hinduism

A religion is practised in one of the three formats—rituals, recitals, and realisation. Hinduism is strictly a religion of realisation that must be attained here and now. It is a different matter that non-spiritual masters of Hinduism make it appear like a religion of recitals and ritual to their followers, even though there is no set of practices that can define Hinduism.

The preceding chapters on scriptures make it clear why Hinduism is neither a regimented religion, nor a proselytising one. The lack of defining boundaries in it makes it difficult to be specific about what Hinduism is, or who is a Hindu. Even a common Hindu is usually not sure what they must do to be a good Hindu. The simple folks believe that it is enough if they follow their family traditions, ceremonies, popular customs, and expensive rituals, while the gullible can't differentiate between corporate religion and true spirituality.

The recent rise of popular Hinduism that seems to concentrate on trivial issues like food, dress, behaviour, etc., is making things more difficult. Impressionable minds fail to breach the frivolous to reach the fundamentals. If this is terrifying to the weak, it is laughable by the indifferent.

has crushed the old moulds forever, and now there is a need for the new that would help a practising Hindu to have a blessed life.

Taking into account the words of past masters, present situation, and the future growth, the new ideals for India would probably be based on these four that may be taken up individually and also collectively.

- Vidya: One should dedicate oneself to some branch of knowledge and strive to be the best in that field, which can be anything, starting from the art of cleaning to the study of the most abstruse subjects. The crux lies in becoming the best to the extent that the practitioner becomes one with that knowledge.

- Sampad: One may go for creating wealth for the nation through business, or other means. The Vaishyas of earlier times were dedicated to making money, but unlike today's money makers, their goal was not to hoard money but to regulate it in the society.

- Seva: Those who cannot do either of the above two, for them service to others is the ideal. Service is not charity in which one feels superior, rather, it is like mother's care in which both mother and child become blessed. *Manusmriti* says, 'Both he who respectfully receives, and he who respectfully makes it, go to heaven. If it is contrary, then they both enter the hell (IV. 235).'

- Tyaga: India is the land of Brahma Vidya, dedicating oneself to self-realisation. So, the goal of every practising Hindu has to be to someday take up this ideal as the way of life. Since God and the world cannot stay together, the men of God have to be established in complete *tyaga* (renunciation), irrespective of which spiritual path they take.

A more elaborate code of conduct needs to be written that would keep the spiritual ideals of Hinduism intact, and also accommodate these four ideals in them.

Will Hinduism remain relevant in the future?

Will Hinduism be able to parry the attacks of science and atheism? Will it even remain relevant? These are some of the unspoken and also the outspoken questions making rounds in and through the cyber world. In fact, questions are being raised about the very relevance of religion. What is the use of religion, they ask, when one can live peacefully without it and wait for death that would end one's existence forever?

If religion has come to be equated with violence in recent times, Hinduism is invariably tagged with ideas like cow worship, elaborate rituals, fossilised customs, and fantastic stories of gods and goddesses. Further, why should one even adhere to a belief system that can't treat its fellow religionists as equals?

The answer to these lie in the earlier chapters. Religion, particularly Hinduism, is not a product of thought process to serve as crutches to lean upon during bad times. Religion is a living experience that makes one perceive the intrinsic nature of the world, beyond its empirical value. A child loves sweets, and a diabetic person is wary of them. These perceptions are due to the empirical value of the sweets, coloured by the subjective needs of a person. The intrinsic nature of sweets is sweetness, beyond the reach of one's subjective demands of seeking it or avoiding it. The role of true religion lies in stripping away the enamels of the world, and then revealing its intrinsic nature of oneness with the divine.

There can be no doubt that not many people would be interested in this lofty ideal, but there would always be some who want to know the eternal behind the non-eternal, and the truth behind the appearance. Religion will always remain relevant for such people who are the true 'salt of the earth'. These are the people to whom the world turns to when it is scorched by the searing heat of materialism that results in tears and helplessness. These are the saints who never say no to the demands of the burdened, and who never fail to bring smile on the face of the failed.

Hindu spiritual ideals being impersonal, these will always continue to shine in all its majesty to bring blessedness in the lives of its saints, and to bring succour to the common man through these saints. The impersonal ideals also imply that these will help bring peace and blessedness to anyone who follows these principles, irrespective of the religion or the society to which one may belong.

The Vedic sages were contributing to the corpus of spiritual ideals thousands of years before Jesus was born as the saviour of the Christian world. *Ramayana* and *Mahabharata* were composed more than a 1,000 years before Lord Buddha opened the spiritual treasures to the whole of Asia. When Alexander reached the banks of Indus riding on his victories, he wanted to take some Brahmins for Aristotle, as asked by the great philosopher. In an anecdotal episode, one Brahmin scoffed at the spiritual ignorance of the conqueror. When threatened with death, the Brahmin laughed at him, saying he was atman that knows no birth and no death! The law of Manu and the treatise on politics by Chanakya were more than 300 years old when the Roman cohorts led by Julius Caesar conquered Europe to come up with the adage 'all roads lead to Rome'. That was the time when the British were still painting their bodies and living the life of the barbarians. Aryabhatta had come up with his idea of zero in mathematics half a millennium before Arabia would wake up to the idea of gathering knowledge. The list goes on.

All this did not deter the powerful from attacking the Hindu race that gloated on its greatness, and preferred ennui that comes from the complacence born of basking in the glory of one's ancestors. The resulting bloodshed, loot and conversion made the Hindus withdraw to the safety of submissiveness the way a tortoise withdraws its limbs when in danger. The consequence, although inevitable, has been a pathetic time warp for the Hindu race.

All this is changing now. The giant tortoise is once again smelling safety, and so it is bringing out its huge limbs to float in the free waters of thought world. The spiritual stagnation resulting from the twin bondages of recitals and rituals has been removed by Sri Ramakrishna, and the social stagnation has been cleaned by democracy and science. Hinduism is once again free, free to be what it is, and free to disseminate the ideals for which it stands.

Attacks on its ideals and principles are nothing new for Hinduism. In the section on philosophy it was discussed how Charvak, the Indian materialists not only attacked the ideals, but came down to outright abusing the practitioners. Buddhism, Jainism, Islam, Christianity, and atheism have all been attacking the principles of Hinduism for thousands of years without being able to create a dent in it.

In an interesting observation, the French traveller Louis Rousselet, in his book *L'Inde des Rajahs* (published in 1876), translated as *India and Its Native Princes—Travels in Central India and in the Presidencies of Bombay and Bengal*, mentioned the following:

Is there a people in the world more tolerant than this good gentle Hindoo people, who have been so often described to us as cunning, cruel and even bloodthirsty? Compare them for an instant with the Mussulmans, or even with ourselves, in spite of our reputation for civilization and tolerance. Only let a Chinese or an Indian come and walk in our streets during a religious festival or ceremony, and will not the crowd exhibit the most hostile feelings towards him if his bearing should not be in conformity with the customs of the country? Will his ignorance excuse him? I doubt it. And in what country could such a spectacle be witnessed as that which met my eyes that day in this square of Benares? There, at ten paces from all that the Hindoo holds to be most sacred in religion, between the Source of Wisdom and the idol of Siva a Protestant missionary has taken his stand beneath a tree. Mounted on a chair, he was preaching in the Hindostani language, on the Christian religion and the errors of paganism. I heard his shrill voice, issuing from the depths of a formidable shirt-collar, eject these words at the crowd, which respectfully and attentively surrounded him— 'You are idolaters! That block of stone which you worship has been taken from a quarry, it is no better than the stone of my house.'

The reproaches called forth no murmur; the missionary was listened to immovably, but his dissertation was attended to, for every now and then one of the audience would put a question, to which the brave apostle replied as best he could. Perhaps we should be disposed to admire the courage of the missionary if the well-known toleration of the Hindoos did not defraud him of all his merit; and it is this tolerance that most disheartens the missionary one of whom said to me 'Our labours are in vain; you can never convert a man who has sufficient conviction in his own religion to listen, without moving a muscle, to all the attacks you can make against it.' (*Swami Vivekananda in the West: New Discoveries*).

One can attack a thing that is limited in time and space, but how can one attack an idea that is timeless and not dependent on any person? If such an idea is attacked at some place, it immediately manifests in some other place in a different form. This is true of every branch of knowledge, including religion. Hinduism is no exception.

The imagined attack on Hinduism by science is more interesting. Not many realise that science has helped Hinduism and its major philosophy Vedanta stand tall amidst the debris of most religious beliefs demolished by the rationality of science. If there is one religion that can never be shaken by any advancement of science, it is Hinduism, and if there is a religious philosophy that is going to pass the test of rationality, it is Vedanta. Being impersonal, it is beyond the attacks of rationality, which is after all a mere mind game limited in time-space duality.

The exclusiveness born of fear and submissiveness is crumbling down to make way for the grand inclusiveness that is the true nature of Hindu religion. After all, God does not dictate the trivialities of life, and hence these are as transient as the passing whiff of wind. Ultimately it is God and the spiritual life that alone matters in Hinduism. The rapid growth of globalisation and universal citizenship cannot afford to live with the idea of exclusiveness, be that in market, or in religion.

So, Hinduism, the religion of inclusiveness, is here to stay in spite of its taboos and totems, rituals and customs, gods and goddesses, cow worship and rat worship, monkey God and elephant God. Some of its customs, practices and rituals are changing, and these may change further, but Hinduism being a palimpsest, nothing gets thrown away here, and so probably most practices would continue to be there, even if in modified forms.

The inner peace that comes to a practising Hindu, and the message of universal peace that comes from the Hindu philosophy, are things that can neither be ignored by a person, nor by the world.

This is living Hinduism.

Select Bibliography

Basu, M. Fundamentals of the Philosophy of Tantra. India: Mira Basu Publisher, 1983.

Biruni, Muhammad ibn Ahmad. *Alberuni's India*. London: Kegan Paul, Trench, Trübner & Co., 1910.

Bose, A.C. *The Call of the Vedas*. Bharatiya Vidya Bhavan. Delhi: Bharatiya Vidya Bhavan, 1999.

Burke, Marie Louis. *Swami Vivekananda in the West: New Discoveries*. Vols I to VI. Mayavati: Advaita Ashrama.

Chatterjee, K.C. *Vedic Selections*. Calcutta: Calcutta University, 1944.

Chatterjee, S.C. and D.M. Dutta. *An Introduction to Indian Philosophy*. Calcutta: Calcutta University Press. 1939.

Griffith, Ralph T.H. *The Rig Veda*. Digireads.com, 2013.

Kaviraj, G. *Selected Writings of M. M. Gopinath Kaviraj*. M.M. Gopinath Kaviraj Centenary Celebrations Committee, 1990.

Keay, J. *India: A History*. India: Harper Press, 2010.

Majumdar, R.C. (ed.). *The History and Culture of the Indian People*. Vols. I to VII, India: Bharatiya Vidya Bhavan, 2001.

Renou, L. *Vedic India*. Indological Books House, 1971.

Stevenson, Ian. *Where Reincarnation and Biology Intersect*. Connecticut, US: Praeger Publishers, 1997.

Valmiki Maharshi. *Shrimad Valmiki Ramayana.* Gorakhpur: Gita Press.

Vivekananda, Swami. *Complete Works.* Mayavati: Advaita Ashrama.

Woodroffe. Sir John. *Mahanirvana Tantra.* South Dakota, US: NuVision Publications, 2007.

Zaehner, R.C. *Hindu Scriptures.* India: Everyman's Library, 1992.

Cultural Heritage of India, vols. I to VI. Kolkata: RKM Institute of Culture, 2006

Manusmriti. Varanasi: Chowkhamba Sanskrit Sansthan, 1997

Rgveda-Samhita (with commentaries from Sayana). Varanasi: Chowkhambha Vidya Bhavan, Varanasi, 2003

Sarva Darshan Samgrah. Varnanasi: Chowkhambha Vidya Bhavan, Varanasi, 2008

Shrimad Bhagavad Gita—Shankara Bhasya. Gorakhpur: Gita Press, 2008

The Complete Mahabharata, vols. I to VI. Gorakhpur: Gita Press, 2003

Note: All citations from the Scriptures follow the convention of representing the book, followed by the hymn number, mantra number, and page number, as follows: (*RV*,I.12.13).

Acknowledgements

Some work can be completed only by the will of Lord. This is one of them. Knowing the limits of my knowledge, I can confidently say that it would have been impossible for me to come up with this mammoth work without the divine hand guiding me. So, I offer my all to him.

Many monks of the Ramakrishna Mission have helped me immensely in completing this work, and also as personal friends. My pranams and thanks to them.

The manuscript of this book was read and re-read by a number of my good friends who also helped me with invaluable suggestions and corrections. Of them, the more involved ones were—Sri Rusi C. Mithawala (Mumbai), Sri Pradipto Chakraborty, Sri Rajshekhar (Chandigarh), Sri Biswanath Bose, Sri Amit Ray Chowdhury, Sri Avinash Singh, Sri Dibyajyoti Chatterjee (Mumbai), Sri Aniruddha Putatunda, Sri M. M. Tewari (Zurich), and Mr Dripta Sarkar (Dublin/Oxford). Thank you all for being with me. You all deserve individual thanks, but lack of space prevents me from doing it.

Sri Nripendra Prasanna Acharya, a great scholar of Hinduism, went through the manuscript meticulously and made important suggestions. His enthusiasm for this work has been infectious, and his kind words of encouragement have been invaluable.

The initial suggestion to write this work came from Ms VK Karthika, the then chief editor at HarperCollins. She had also been kind enough to accept four books of mine for the house. More than all this, I hold her in great esteem for her scholarship, and for moulding the literary careers of many authors.

Ms Debasri Rakshit, the point person for my works at M/S HarperCollins, drove me towards completing this work. Mr Pranav Kumar Singh and Sri Hersh Bharadwaj, both of them from publishing world, and my very good friends, have been very appreciative of this work. Their support during crucial phases of this work helped it move significantly. Thanks to all of them.

Sri Ajey Ranade, IPS, came as a whiff of fresh wind in my personal and literary life. A great friend, his contribution in this work is simply immense, and his continued support is beyond words of thanks.

Dr. Shyam Anand Jha, Muzaffarpur, who is associated with management teaching, has been a great help in innumerable ways in my life and in the production of this work. Thank you, Shyam ji.

Sri Nirmal Kanti Bhattacharjee, Director Niyogi Books, was kind enough to go through the manuscript and accept it for publication. I am grateful to him for his kindness. Ms Jayalakshmi Sengupta, the editor of this book, has worked very hard on it to give it an excellent finish. She very patiently bore with my quirks and accommodated my demands to complete the job, which two earlier editors had failed to do. Thank you, Jaya ji.

To end, I wish to thank Sri Ajay Nayak, IAS, who has been a great inspiration behind all my works. Scholarly, humble, and considerate, he has been my sustaining force over the years. He is also responsible for prodding me into writing through his constant coaxing.

Index